Editing – 10 Steps

Editing – 10 Steps

Write, read, and then edit to successfully submit all types of writing to audiences.

Bonny Franke

authorHOUSE®

AuthorHouse™
1663 Liberty Drive
Bloomington, IN 47403
www.authorhouse.com
Phone: 1 (800) 839-8640

Published by AuthorHouse 03/18/2015

ISBN: 978-1-4969-6885-2 (sc)
ISBN: 978-1-4969-6884-5 (e)

Library of Congress Control Number: 2015902007

Print information available on the last page

Any people depicted in stock imagery provided by Thinkstock are models,
and such images are being used for illustrative purposes only.
Certain stock imagery © Thinkstock.

This book is printed on acid-free paper.

TABLE OF CONTENTS

PREFACE

Writers Anonymous originated as a discussion group for the purpose of refining the writings of people with different levels of experience when trying to complete their work and/or have their individual works published.

Dr. Bonny Franke initiated and coordinated the meetings in which she provided written guides to facilitate the group's involvement. <u>*EDITING*–10 Steps</u> came out of the discussions. The process of asking Dr. Franke to edit manuscripts surfaced among the major needs of the varied and talented people who participated in the *Writers Anonymous* gatherings. The different types of writing she edited for members of the group included first-time manuscripts, historical novels, and screen plays.

Barnes and Noble, in Dallas and Plano, were kind enough to sponsor regular weekly meetings over a four-year period for the *Writers Anonymous* discussion groups. Barnes and Noble's gracious supply of announcements, signs, and designated space were greatly appreciated.

Alisha Byerly, a graduate of Texas Woman's University with a Bachelor's degree in World Literature provided a fresh approach as the editing guide evolved. The critical questions she asked as an external critic were major assets. Thank you, Alisha.

INTRODUCTION

Writer as Editor

When a writer conceives of a story to be told, or begins the process of writing a book, the multiple stages required for completion are daunting. Both new and experienced writers recognize that a solitary demanding effort is required to push the initial idea through to completion.

Each step in the writing, revising, improving process benefits from cautions that help writers avoid pitfalls or disappointments. Many common errors found in any level of writing are included as part of <u>Editing – 10 Steps</u> which gives specifics as to how one can improve the objective editing of their own work.

<u>Editing – 10 Steps</u> is intended to provide reminders to writers who want to make their various styles and levels of experience come alive. Is this a writers' guide? It is not intended to be, but perhaps it will assist writers capture the incentive needed to proceed during the multiple revision and polishing stages necessary for actual completion of any work.

Phillip Margolin wrote: *"I don't know about other authors, but I need a good editor to take my first draft and made it into a book that can be published."* – <u>Supreme Justice</u>, Harper, 2011, p. 388.

Chapter One

Grammar Edits

"A good book is never written. It is re-written."

- William Faulkner

First drafts are usually hurry-up documents meant only to capture a theme or the intent of a story. Enthusiastic speed is admirable. Ignoring quality through hurry tactics is not advisable. Caution signs can prevent errors prompted by a variety of attitudes on the part of the writer. When psychobabble takes over, or the writing appears to be only a stream of consciousness, a plot and its components suffer.

Written as quickly as possible to keep continuity within the framework of the story, initial efforts are rarely adequate manuscripts. Some writers try to start out by finishing and ponder over each word. This approach usually frustrates the writer and seldom satisfies the editor. First drafts are merely first efforts and are not expected to be finished products. Plots take twists and evolve with expanded scenes and complicated people who interrupt actions and delay intentions of even the best of writers. Too much examination of the first words put to paper during an initial draft may result in a tight and refined beginning that folds into a thwarted effort. Every draft needs polish throughout without constant reviews of just the first few pages.

Polish includes looking for unintended errors, gaps, or duplications. When polished by the writer or suggested by editing, some descriptions are expanded or inserted where none were included before. The caution here is to avoid stuffing some sections and letting other sections lay bare. Not all writers or editors recognize that a passage or a phrase can be replaced by something better.

Some writers resist allowing changes to be made. *It is written! It must be kept!* Insistence that a group of words are so important or so well written that there is no way improvements can be made is not uncommon. The refusal to see that changes need to be made reflects an attitude which can be difficult to overcome, but changes may be necessary to improve a written statement. An editor who is alert to resistance may be able to find an alternative approach to language improvements, but only if the attitude of being resistant is recognized by both editor and writer.

The writer may resist change or want to keep the precious words out of some error of judgment or some need that impedes the process of making improvements. Myopic writers who do not want a single word or punctuation mark deleted or changed, are set on a long road to despair. With many forms of language available, skilled writers know their options and the approach best suited to their story. Each piece of writing undergoes corrections, eliminations, substitutions, and expansions of scenes and action. Or, at least, it should.

Organization, style, integration of events with story, character identifications, and distractions are components of content, but little grammar mistakes can make the whole process come unglued. Many professional writers may not know the rules of grammar, but they know the rule applications and how to craft meaningful works. Grammar is a tool used to communicate the written thought. Editors depend upon the support of grammar, the underpinnings of substance in writing. Grammar edits require knowing what constitutes grammatical accuracies without having to be personally acquainted with gerunds or knowing when a participle need not dangle. Skilled writers know how to form impressive plots. They know how to keep dialogue simple enough to enrich a scene, and to show the vagaries among the people included in a story.

Revisions to any form of writing may be mechanical or substantive. Any group of words may need grammatical adjustments, or they may need to have the meaning revised. Grammar corrections are relatively easy to make, but changes in meaning always require objectivity and persistence. Writer attitudes may need to be adjusted, timelines may have to be shifted, and aggravations may have to be set aside. For most people, change is difficult to master. New approaches to solving any problem demand that selfish aggrandizements be set aside and personal egos forgotten if success is to be warranted.

The audience is the ultimate critic. The writer is the communicator. The message is clear or unclear. The intent is to inform or to entertain, or both. The content is awkward or skilled. The result is either accessible to wide understanding, or leads to misunderstanding. Underlying content difficulties include errors that thwart the pursuit of both clarity and spell-binding progression within a work and require stiff edits.

Copy edits:

Copy edits look for mistakes in spelling, noun to verb use, capitalizations, punctuations, and other inconsistencies that come into play unintentionally. Using incorrect grammar is inexcusable unless improperly used words are intended to convey an ignorant character.

A commonly misused phrase is 'the temperature rose above the century mark.' A century is a span of time of one-hundred years, and does *not* measure temperature. Another misused phrase: "Those robotic figures look just *like us*!" No, they don't. They look just like "*we do*!" thanks to editing that corrected the language. Texts that demonstrate illiteracy are unexpected and disconcerting. Blatant errors need correction during the editing process. Even diligent writers and editors miss some of the small errors that creep through. Copy edits include proofing for language accuracy.

It's hard to read a document when it is single spaced and there is no room to insert comments, or how to mark corrections. Therefore, double spaced is best. There needs to be enough space to insert words, letters, or punctuation. Margins should be wide enough to include punctuation notes, or additional ideas for possible insertion later.

With computers, cuts and pastes are relatively simple to make. When working on a long document, cut and paste changes often get lost. A printed version makes it easier to identify corrections needed. Also, a printout saves material that otherwise might be lost. Thinking ahead to that dream of being published, many agents and publishing houses prefer to receive both computer files and hard copies of any material requested for consideration.

Knowing some proofreading marks are helpful when working on paper documents. When in doubt, page 1687 of Webster's <u>New World Dictionary,</u> <u>Second College Edition</u> has a fully illustrated example of how to do standard proofreading. Another helpful approach is to use a red pen and repeat in the margin what is to be inserted. Commas and periods and other small marks are easily lost when indicated only in the body copy by a black pen.

It is not important to be a lexicographer, or to be an expert in onomatopoeia in order to write well. It is important, however, to know when a sentence or a passage does not fit the story nor belong in the plot.

Content edits:

Content edits include organization and style. Meanings change with the inadvertent use of a wrong word that won't be caught by the computer's 'spell-check.' Many words present choices and reflect a writer's intention. Other words do not. For example, *esthetic* may become *aesthetic;* a Browning pistol may be a called a *hand gun,* a *hand-gun,* or a *handgun.* Choices abound, but continual reviews can eliminate mistakes and avoid the appearance of sloppy work. Overlooking what may or may not be obvious include both misspelled and misplaced words.

Consider the following: *The great <u>steal</u> of Texas hung over the outhouse door.*

He searched for lists of drugs on which patients had expired. (They expired on lists?)

Spelled correctly, a work or a word conveys the meaning intended. Spelled incorrectly, a misspelled word may be dialect, specific to a language pattern to demonstrate a particular country or region, an idiomatic term, or the special language of an individual. But, it could simply be a mistake missed in review. Check it! Be exact in the word's intent and in its appropriate use.

Even a good edit may not discover all of the gremlins who live inside the computer. Computers don't recognize every word, nor do they *flay* (this should be <u>flag</u>) a correctly spelled word that is misplaced or misused. Technology is great, but spell-checker missed the following:

Someone does not *except* an invitation when they want to *accept* it.

One cannot be *effective* in their writing when the word used is *affective.*

When the sections are *all ready,* it is because they are *already* edited. (Both are correct.)

A common error is made when the word *there* is mistaken for *their* or when the word should be *they're.* *A lot* is not one word, although it is frequently typed as one. A keen edit assures that *many*, or *several,* or a finite number is used instead of *a lot.*

One ordinary mistake made by many writers and by computer spell-checks is the difference between the words 'sit' and 'set.' People **sit**. Objects **set**. Almost a twin error is the use of 'lie' and 'lay.' People **lie** down. Objects **lay** where they are placed. *The log house **set** on a hill.*

One dramatic exception to the use of the word 'lie' resides in the world of golf because of the old Scottish dialect now adapted to the modern world. *The golf ball ran into the bunker and left the golfer with a bad **lie.*** The use of the word *lie* is correct in this instance and should not be corrected by edits.

As Walter Winchell said, "Nothing *recedes* like success." Other switched words may include: *Alternation* took place in the *altercation.* The *nickel* was made of *nickle.* Misspelled and incorrectly used words become villains to harass writers and deceive readers. Thoroughness succeeds when every mark on the page is examined with persistence.

One error that frequently invades the best of writing is the use of the little word *as* to mean something other than what it means. The little word **as** does **not** mean while, or when, or since, or like, or because. *As* implies *also, concerning that, so to speak,* and some variations of *the degree* to which something is expected or measured. Editing tries to catch small and large mistakes made *while* writing. Each word is important. If wrongfully used, the misuse of any word can be irritating to editors and to readers. The correct use of **as** in standard proper form is:

He ran **as** fast **as** he could.

As long **as** he could, he ran.

He ran **as** well **as** he could.

As of yet there is no record **as** to his winning.

As a reward, a win was **as** good **as** gold.

Although commonly used incorrectly, misuse of the words *since, with, as, while* and *like,* tempt readers to assume the writer is either lazy or ignorant. Instead of writing "She spoke *as* she closed the door," correctly write: "She spoke *when* she closed the door." Or, write: "She spoke *while* she closed the door."

Check on *this, that, which, these, those,* and *it.* All personal pronouns refer to something or someone. When the meaning can be lost, substitute the noun instead of the pronoun since pronouns can get in the way of clarity. If it is not clear, change it to assure correct language use.

John tossed the beer cans, but she got tired of John's behavior when he tossed beer cans.

Incorrect: "She got tired of <u>him</u> tossing beer cans!"

Adequate: "She got tired of <u>his</u> tossing beer cans!"

Correct: "She got tired of John tossing beer cans!"

Unless poor or broken grammar is used to lend individuality to a character to reflect a social or educational status, then correct grammar is best. There are always exceptions. Formal language is appropriate in formal awards, officials, legal documents and many nonfiction writings. However, the use of strictly proper form usually indicates a non-native speaker or characterizes someone who is a 'stuffed-shirt' or someone who is trying to impress others by using 'high-brow' language.

Slang, foul language, idioms, etc. may sound natural to the writer, but they must be natural to the character represented and also seem natural to the reader. Some off-beat slang distracts and adds little to the plot. Subtle differences between what is necessary and what is filler or distractions can be found when they are specifically sought out during editing. A good edit requires the ability to know how to 'fix' bad or improper language usage that is critical to clarity. Watch your words! As a magician watches the audience, a writer watches meanings which warp or misdirect impressions.

Profanity may be an easy way to highlight a character's thoughts, but must not distract from the story. If necessary, profanity lends color to shady scenes but seldom carries a plot forward. Watch out for excessively foul language. It may be needed and appropriate or may be only intended to shock. The writer or the editor can decide when too much becomes too much. More may be added or more deleted. Cuss words, as they spew from a distinctly unsavory character may add color. Otherwise, profanity may not be necessary.

The politically correct use of *his or her* surrounded writing issues early in the nineteen seventies as did racially loaded or gender biased words. A thorough edit should look for neutral language when biased or foul words add nothing. When exaggerating a character's bias, colorful language styles should be obviously intentional or should be changed to become politically correct and non-offensive.

Punctuation:

Punctuation serves only one purpose: to make intent clear. Clarity and intent benefit from the skillful use of the basic tools of language and both suffer when the basic tools are ignored. Dots (ellipses), dashes, colons, semi-colons, and hyphens should be reserved for their intended uses rather than to prompt the writer to bend to temptation and use them willly-nilly as the muse takes over.

Punctuation marks have substance and specific meanings. The mechanics of placement of commas, periods, etc. either help the reader or they get in the way of understanding what is intended. The many choices made by writers give flexibility and set tone or mood to different approaches in the use of various punctuation marks. Whatever approach is chosen, it should be consistent with the intentions of the writer. It is unacceptable to most people to read a work that shows a highly sophisticated use of punctuation that borders on a classical approach only to be stunned when an inconsistent use of punctuation unexpectedly appears. The watchword here is *consistency.*

In addition to knowing how the strength of good grammar applies, punctuation used may either confuse or clarify. Dashes can be used too often and are unnecessary most of the time. When speed writing is undertaken, as when a letter is dashed off to a friend, the writing allows for random thoughts expressed quickly without the need for formality. When editing a formal, or a more informative piece of writing, a punctuation edit assures that dashes are few and only used when necessary.

Wilson Follett cautioned: "The comma causes trouble equally by its absence, by its presence, and by wrong placement." Commas are controversial. Little commas, like little words, often confuse the use and meaning for which they were intended. Edit a comma in, or edit a comma out, but know which approach best fits, and keep consistency throughout.

Without knowing or relying on all or any grammatical rules that apply to commas, both writer and editor rely on experience or extensive reading to know when and where a comma should appear. If left out when needed, or if inserted wrongly, a comma may create confusion in understanding what is meant.

Short items in a series need commas for clarity. Disagreements occur on whether or not to put a comma after the second in a series or leave it out. Edits for consistency help, but including a comma after the second item in a series is clearer to the reader. Such as in: *'She was tall, skinny, and blond."* When the last comma is omitted, the sentence is: *"She was tall, skinny and blond."* The emphasis shifts by comma use.

Colons and semicolons have separate and distinct reasons for existing. Colons signal that whatever comes afterwards is very important, be it a clause, a phrase, a list, a description, or an idea. The semicolon is a cousin to both commas and periods. A semicolon is weaker than a period, but is stronger than a comma and is used only when there is a more distinct break in a sentence than that indicated by a comma. Some people practice the art of editing by reading aloud each sentence that is questioned and then deciding whether or not a comma, a semicolon, or a colon is misplaced. This process may take longer, but it usually promotes accuracy and clarity.

Prepositions:

Prepositions are necessary, but full of traps. Too many or too much repetitive use of prepositions can lead to unending and unnecessarily foggy writing. Modifiers can be strong allies or dangle precipitously. Too many adjectives or too many pronouns, on the other hand, can be the mark of an amateur. Caution and frugality are advised. Either omitted or misplaced, a modifier often produces humorous or unintentional misunderstanding.

The process of editing involves finding ways to improve on an approach used. The minutia of editing includes knowing when to use or when to avoid rules of language. Incorrect grammar, when used, must be intended. When standard rules of language are ignored, there must be a reason otherwise the reader may become confused or even irritated.

Commonly used words often mystify skilled writers and baffle editors. Some sound plural when they are singular. Consider the following as to the clarity of intention or actual meaning.

Somebody:	Somebody got *their* hair cut. (incorrect)
	Somebody got *his* hair cut.
Each:	Each little girl can take *their* turn. (incorrect)
	Each little girl can take *her* turn.

Anyone:	Anyone can play *their* own way. (incorrect)
	Anyone can play *his or her* own way.
Everyone:	Everyone should take *their* place. (incorrect)
	Everyone should take *his or her* place.
Everybody:	Everybody got *their* own reward. incorrect)
	Everybody got *his or her* own reward.
I versus Me:	He's just *like me.* (incorrect)
	He's just like *I am.*

People who invest in the stock market know '*investing just like me'* ignores the proper use of the phrase '*investing just like I do.'* Major brokerage firms usually reject ads that contain poor grammar in much the same way that publishers reject writing with grammar errors. Use of incorrect grammar may be appropriate according to an uneducated character's image, but it is not acceptable in general narrative since readers expect writers to be literate.

All writers, whether for ad copy or for Congressional delegates, must know the many ways to display a character's ignorance and to illustrate their own intelligence.

Contractions:

Contractions can go unnoticed when correctly used. Unintended errors add confusion if they are not caught and corrected. Errors are made when *I'd've* translates into *I would have, or didn't* is used instead of *did not.* Similarly, *hadn't* does not mean *had not.* The simple approach is to spell out whatever is meant. On and on, the little pieces get in the way of the big idea. When the edit hat goes on, analysis and observations win even if a dictionary is needed.

Articles and Adjectives:

Articles are too frequently misused or omitted, but little words can change the intentions of the writer. Often, *a, an,* and *the* may be overlooked. They each mean something different. Little article *a* means *one and only one.* Little article *the* means *the specific one.*

Adjectives can heighten a sense of place, of time, and of people. Too many adjectives can lead to dullness or be distractions. When the use of adjectives is over-done, many can be cut. Lesson Fourteen of <u>Fiction Writing,</u> Volume III, p. 239 (Famous Writers School, Westport, Conn. 1960) includes a quote from Mark Twain written to a schoolboy in 1880.

"I notice that you use plain, simple language, short words and brief sentences. That is the way to write English—it is the modern way, and the best way. Stick to it; don't let fluff and flowers and verbosity creep in. When you catch adjectives, kill most of them—then the rest will be valuable. They weaken when they are too frequent and close together; they give strength when they are sparsely used and wide apart. An adjective habit, or a wordy, diffuse or flowery habit, once fastened upon a person, is as hard to get rid of as any other vice."

One good adjective will suffice to make the point, otherwise redundancy clouds the picture. Compare the following:

It's *a <u>usual</u> custom* but a <u>*final*</u> *outcome* was based on <u>*past*</u> *history* and <u>*surrounding*</u> *circumstance* and *the <u>old</u> adage* that <u>*absolute*</u> *proof* was needed to come up with a <u>*general decision*</u> with data provided by an <u>*inexperienced*</u> *novice.*

All customs are <u>usual</u>. Outcomes are <u>final</u>. History re-counts the <u>past.</u> Circumstances <u>surround.</u> Adages are <u>old</u>. Proof stands <u>absolute</u>, and decisions are <u>final</u>, or <u>specific</u>, but not <u>general</u>. An <u>inexperienced</u> novice is redundant since all novices are inexperienced.

Prepositions:

Prepositions usually move toward a passive mode and may not be intentional. Editors watch for propositional phrases, adjective over-use, and other windy approaches that can be tightened and strengthened. When the tendency is to use a phrase such as '*in advance of considering such excessively warped viewpoints which come into play,*' substitute '*before thinking about warped attitudes.*'

Too many prepositions cloud meaning and shorter is clearer. "The Board of Trustees, *in* which there was little interaction *of the* various personalities and *of which* there was vast differences *with* conflicting agendas, the problems grew *with* slim hope for resolution."

The same statement can be turned into action (with no negative criticism) when written as: "Limited interaction between Board members interfered with problem resolutions due to conflicting agendas among the members."

If intended to show a pompous situation, leave it. Otherwise, change it to fit the action needed. When doubt about cutting long sentences enters into the process, consider using new terms or more current phrases.

The list of new terms that came into use during and after the industrial revolution is long and varied. The space age introduced more changes. The computer or technology decades brought different terms into vogue. The use of technical terms need not limit a story to an audience of specialized experts but can include the general reader who may or may not have a technical background but expects to understand what is meant.

Times change and language changes when new terms take on new and different meanings. 'Refrigerators' were once 'ice boxes' because they were intended to hold blocks of ice which cooled perishable foods. 'Kodax' eventually became an ordinary term used to refer to any and all cameras. "Kleenex' became a substitute for paper tissues which began to replace handkerchiefs which were often known as 'hankies.'

Some valid words have been dropped from ordinary use altogether, or their meanings have evolved. 'You will *rue* the day!' or, 'you'll *regret* it!' 'The *travail* of collecting the *offal* was *pellucid.*' Or, '*it was clear that collecting trash was hard work.*' If the story is about the Viking, Goths, Knights, or other ancient peoples, the words *habergeon* or *hauberk* may refer to short, sleeveless garb of protective mail. Children once learned to do their *ciphers,* which originally referred to *a zero* but came to refer to *numbers*, and then *codes* and then to *solving problems in arithmetic.* Cipher contests are still held for those who want a challenge in solving arithmetic problems.

Most words with obscure meanings can be simply stated. A small game often played by travelers on long road trips is called *Stinky Pinkie,* the meaning of which is '*perfumed little finger.*' What does a '*revenue enhancement program for mobilization*' mean? It's a '*gas tax.*' '*A multiple citizenry mobile transference*' is a '*bus.*' And so on. Keep it fun but avoid gobbledygook.

Another set of jargon is job-speak. Some meaning gets lost or falls prey to unique professional terms such as those used in legalese. An entire vocabulary comes attached to each professional discipline and boundless hours are spent learning specific terms that have little meaning outside individual jobs. Unless a professional text is being prepared for a specialized audience, use terms or explanations that clearly convey the meaning of each word. (*Utilized* could be the term used here, but *utilized* simply means *used.*)

Redundant expressions and padded phrases add little to keep a story moving. Forget the extra padding in an effort to lengthen the story. '*During the course of*' means '*while*' or perhaps it means '*during.*' '*On a theoretical level*' usually means '*in theory.*' People '*are in the neighborhood,*' or they can be '*close by*' or simply '*near.*' The ordinary word '*together*' can replace '*assembled*' or '*joined*' or '*merged*' or '*combined*' when simplicity is needed. The little word '*twice*' can replace the phrase '*on two separate occasions.*' Substitute '*most*' for 'the *majority of.*' Try out the fact that readers '*consider*' good stories when they buy a book, instead of they '*take into consideration*' the plot when buying a book.

The books were not cataloged '*as to*' author and subject, but '*by*' author and subject. The students were not housed '*as to*' age and gender, but '*by*' age and gender. Tightening sentences can be done by choice or by accident, but shorter sentences and phrases make both pace and suspense easier reading. Brevity is better when there is an effort to convey action.

Writers who are careful of present or past tenses know when they use the active voice that the person who is the subject of the verb has taken action. They also know that whatever or whomever received the action is demonstrated by the passive voice. Examples: He did it (active). It was done to him (passive). Grammar is important. Intent is vital. Both in writing and in editing, the intent must be clear to the reader. Active versus passive verbs change the moods intended.

A sweep of a finished or almost finished first draft helps assure that grammar is used as a tool with which to communicate, that all types of grammatical errors are caught, and each sentence is as it was intended. Avoid rushing in order to produce a more polished draft.

CHAPTER TWO

Points Of View

Books create pictures in readers' minds.

-B. Franke

A point of view (often called 'voice') is not as confusing as sometimes claimed. Must there be only one? Critics disagree on what constitutes the proper use of voice, what is in vogue, and even what is the best approach to use in different genres as a tale is woven to its best advantage.

Styles change and rules change over time. Writing that was expected and acceptable decades ago is ignored by some popular writers of the twenty-first century. The editing process has evolved over the past decades as well, and editors now look for writers' intentions among the different points of view used as well as possible reader reactions to the completed document. Challenges are never in short supply.

Editing a work requires specific examinations and answers to oblique questions such as: What grammatical 'voice' is best for the work? Is the work intended to be instructional? Does the voice chosen add to the intended story? Other questions may arise during editing, but all questions serve as a guide to thoroughness.

In literary fiction it has been expected that writers pick one voice and stay with it consistently throughout in order to meet a standard of professionalism. In both literary and commercial fictions, however, writers can use a combination of points of view to add more complexity to the story. Editors are aware that multiple points of view add variety, increase the options of changing scenes or settings, and can create either emotional affinity or distance between characters and readers.

An editor looks at a point of view and determines that it best reflects the story being told, or not. Both writers and editors may use guidelines to check on the appropriate voice being used. There are several categorical genres which ordinarily influence the voice chosen.

<u>How-to</u> or <u>Instructional Guides</u> usually present direct statements in the second person.

<u>Autobiographical</u> essays or books ordinarily use the first person.

General topic <u>Essays</u> vary but may use the first person, second person, or third person.

<u>Poetry</u> focuses on touching the mysteries of experiences and insights and the voice is particular to the topic.

<u>Drama</u> relies heavily on conversations to carry the mood, the action, and the intent of the story being told. All voices and tenses may be necessary to explain and convey the messages inherent or implied in the drama.

<u>Screen plays</u>, or <u>Made-for-TV </u>scripts are a mix of dialogues and instructions.

<u>Non-fiction</u> ordinarily depends upon the third person to establish authority and to provide information.

Fiction expands the options available to the writer. Persuasive and action plots support intensity in the voices chosen. Literary fiction uses more formal language while commercial fiction allows more flexibility and familiarity in both speech patterns and the use of mixed voices. Dual or multiple points of view may be used when the thoughts of two or more significant characters are included. Points of view may shift when different people make different contributions to the story. Mixed or multiple points of view become a challenge to editing since consistency can be lost or become distorted When more than one person's thoughts are included, the thoughts have to be distinct from each other in order for the reader to keep the people separated.

Separate points of view can be difficult to write and even more challenging to edit. The effective separation approach puts multiple people into individual mind sets and offers the writer an opportunity to display a variety of personality types as the story unfolds. Short sentences when different people are speaking add punch to the dialogue.

Check to assure that consistency of use reflects the mood or degree of action is exactly what is intended. When a time sequence changes because mistakes were made by switching from a present tense to a past or a future tense, errors are noticeable. Sequences in time are demonstrated by use of active voice verbs. Even experienced writers and editors lose track of when or where something takes place, but editing both time and location consistency can help avoid contradictions.

Passive verbs, whether light or serious, can be stumbling blocks to action and clarity of intent. The passive voice may come across as convoluted plodding.

The 'to be' forms: *is, am, are, was, were, be, been, being,* are passive and used as needed. When strung together, passive forms become villains to impede and smother pace. Passive words invite dull work and staid readings, but words can be changed during the editing process and crisp, active reading can emerge.

Choices made before, during, and after writing a piece include checks to see if changes in points of view were intentional or accidental. Switches between passive or active voice can remain or they can be changed. When lively movements are intended, active voice improves clarity and pace, but action terms are not always appropriate to mood or attitudes desired.

Types of voice:

Some of the following may be used as guides:

First Person: *Me, my, myself, and I* tell the story and set the approach used throughout. Language, however, can vary when using the first person. The "I" who tells the story has to stay alive and interesting (unless the plot includes a zombie) but doesn't have to be a gutter-talker (unless *my* dwelling is in the gutter or *I* only know how to use foul language). Exceptions are everywhere, but consistency is paramount.

A first person approach limits the writer to one person's point of view, usually that of the lead character. Continuity is critical. The character's personality or opinions must belong to only one person with interesting dialogue, friends, attitudes, and movements. There should be descriptions of body-type, color of hair, length of coats worn, or other identifications included that separate one person from another in order to avoid confusion among readers.

When a long piece of writing is set in a first person point of view, the story becomes limited to one person's perspective on places seen and events that take place. While the first person point of view is intimate and allows each thought or pain to be expressed, there is danger in holding all of the various characters to one perspective. Autobiographical writing may be the exception when other people's religious, social, or philosophical perspectives are constricted by the perception of the person who is documenting the autobiography. Other characters have to be involved even when a story is cast in the first person. It's difficult to create more than one exciting character or involve more than one person who needs to be fully developed when writing involves only the first person point of view. Limits put on one person's descriptions, combined with a need to involve many people in a story, alters choices of how many characters are included. First person use is interesting, but can be difficult when not used skillfully and carefully edited.

One way to overcome a limited point of view is through groups of people who help tell the story when they talk to each other. Others who are included should be described earlier in the manuscript and their personalities established. Strangers cannot suddenly appear but must be explained or the story gets muddled and readers get disappointed.

Group points of view often use the first person plural to broaden the style and avoid limiting the story to one person's perspective. *"We did that. But we didn't really change our minds, did we?"* Group opinions can be shown in a direct quote of agreement, such as *"Yeah, Bud. Let's all go!"* For the most part, the group approach is used to move the story forward or to move the action from one place or another, or simply to add variety.

Skill levels apparently improve when the use of "I" in speaking, in writing, and editing is eliminated. With good writing and solid editing at stake, the focus shifts away from the solitary person and includes others.

Second Person:

You are the person who gets inside the reader's head when the tricky second person style is used. Advertising copy makes good use of the 'second person' voice since the main purposes of ads is to instill confidence in the product and to appeal to a purchaser. In manuals intended to be instructional or to use as operational guides effectively use the second person because 'you' are the one intended to perform whatever task is included in the manuals. 'You must do. You must not do' are instructional statements. Repetitions may softly guide a reader toward an accomplishment. 'I don't know how' is counter-productive. 'You don't know how?' can be encouragement. Encouragement and guidance toward accomplishments through repetitions are valid in instructional or educational materials.

An editing dilemma is to find too many, or in some cases not enough, repetitions. Actually counting how many times the same word or the same phrase appears may guide corrections that need to be made. When there is too much repetition, change the words, revise the sentences, or delete the section unless it is critical to understanding what is being repeated.

In the second person point of view, the reader can identify with the lead character and can even become directly involved with various other characters. It is somewhat unusual for an entire novel to be written in the second person, but there are advantages. When readers are addressed directly, they feel more involved in the story. Edits look for ways to elicit positive reactions to whatever message is intended and adjust any approach that may disenchant readers or not completely engage them.

The point of view used reflects attitude, conveys humor or angst, and affects the timing of actions taken. Some critics of commercial fiction (as opposed to literary fiction) find the extensive use of second person point of view as sensationalizing and too flippant to be taken seriously. More readily acceptable in classical styles of literary fiction, second person point of view facilitates identifying with strong characters.

Morality stories were once widely told and were frequent subject matter for beginner and advanced writers since contact with others in broader communities was either impossible or infrequent. Readers responded well to being 'talked to' through various lengthy novels that addressed them directly. In the twenty-first century, readers are less patient and tend to lose interest rather quickly due to the rapid pace of advancing technologies.

As long as the editing process includes an awareness of any confusion that can surround use of the second person point of view, there are many positives. Intimacy can be displayed, force of motives can be demonstrated, and connections between acts and results can be subtle or obvious. Personal involvement on the part of the reader is the key to successfully writing and editing use of the second person point of view.

Third Person:

The ghost in the corner sees *her, him, them,* and *they.* Writing that distinguishes ideas, locations, people, and events helps cement the approach used. Third person writing is easier than a first or second person perspective, but has its pitfalls. Third person objectivity may limit character development or stifle adventures intended to broaden a story.

Combined or mixed points of view add interest. First person perspectives usually shift into second person when comments are direct quotes. Different observers may give various or conflicting reports of the same event. Mismatched accounts don't change the point of view of different observers. Instead, there are only different statements according to how each person reports the same happening.

By integrating observations made by one character or another, emotions or attitudes can be added. What different characters see or feel combined with acts and results all contribute to enriched scenes. External observations can mix with personal thoughts or silent wishes.

In either external or internal third person points of view, the writer's point of view or opinions can be disguised and not easily discernable. The editor has to look for writer bias phrases that seep into sentences and spoil the story. It becomes the editor's task to propose either changes or deletions. One approach to strengthening such a section is to let dialogue carry the action instead of leaving in descriptive narrative that may be only an aside that the writer has to get into a story in order to lengthen a manuscript.

Third person mixed:

Many writers separate the third person approach into variations of multiple or combination of point of view. Occasionally, an intermingling of first, second, or third person approaches are used when times or situations have changed. Bouncing back and forth between what is happening and how one or more characters feel about what's going on can mean a change to a different point of view. Finding out how different characters feel about their plight depends on how different points of view are used and how insights are presented. When (or if) alternative approaches in voice are included, the result must be clear, clear, clear!

Whether used as external observation of factual description and events or inclusive of thoughts, dreams, internal angst or perspectives, the third person point of view can be varied. Multiple points of view include many characters. There are differences between multiple and combined points of view. Some writers use both. Editors know the differences and look for distractions that come from the way a writer uses one view or another. Combined points of view means using both what is seen or thought by various characters throughout the plot and its multiple twists and turns. With a natural shift in perspective, words or perceptions add either quiet flavor or heightened excitement to a scene.

If the writer does not inject a clear explanation, or if the voices used get muddled, it may become the job of the editor to help clarify intentions without doing a re-write. It may be sufficient for an edit to simply point out some of the confusing factors. Mixing the points of view may confuse the reader. The writer/editor's task is to recognize inappropriate mixture and make adjustments.

Internal Point of View:

Use of third person point of view varies. When each character's thoughts and feelings are displayed, motives and behaviors are better explained and perhaps better understood. That does not mean that every little anger or frustration should be recorded nor does it mean that every twinge of feeling should be included. Edit out babble unless it confirms a character's background, personality, or motive to twist fate.

Some writers employ a stream-of-consciousness approach to demonstrate internal existence and an internal point of view. William Faulkner's <u>Light in August</u> and <u>As I Lay Dying</u> both reveal hidden thoughts and exploit inner motives in tangled webs of quirks and private obsessions. James Joyce used a first person tactic that avoided all punctuations to illustrate his notion of how internal thinking and feelings can be communicated to readers.

Monologues are often performed on stage or inserted in fiction as ways to explain motives and reactions to the behavior of others. Monologues can represent self-focused first voice dialogue or explore reactions to various situations. The wide variety of approaches used to illustrate internal existence is not limited to a few examples. Edits helps determine when the approach is valid. Interest can be maintained as long as the approach used is reliable and effective and does not allow the characters to fall into dull reminiscing.

External Point of View:

If only external appearances, actions, or physical features are given, the point of view is external only and the internal existence of characters may not be known.

The external point of view has a lot of restrictions. Major among the constraints is to avoid including deep psychological or social motives or interpretations of various deeds. The emphasis here in on the depth of mental or emotional insights included, not on the frequency of shallow mentions.

The onus of comprehending the meaning of the total work falls to the reader when a strictly external point of view is used. The edit of such work can be a challenge in itself. Alertness of intent and awareness of consistency is critical and must be communicated to the reader. Flavor, subtle innuendos, mystery, and flawless achievements call for imaginative observations that are objective and plainly outside the mental chaos of any of the characters. This means both writer and editor need to be alert for clear meaning and not allow obscure ramblings to sneak into the story either through dialogue or narrative.

When people think, they usually talk. Some talk without thinking. The approach used depends on the writer and the characters involved. When limited to an external point of view, writers depend on dialogues to explore meanings deeper than those conveyed strictly by outward appearance or circumstance. Editing by cutting what is out of place or confusing makes both the dialogue and the people talking come across as more believable. Each character should stay consistent to whatever image they are supposed to project, but no person included in the story should have to be lifeless or colorless to the point that personalities are bland.

Combinations of both internal and external points of view are common in mystery and crime stories. Villains or heroes may have either an internal or an external point of view in a mixed combination in the same story. Shifts in perspective between different characters can take place at different levels of sophistication or presentation but shifts in voice stays consistent.

There can be more than one witness to the same event, but each person may describe the event differently and from their individual perspective. The note-taker who records the witnesses' statements uses the same approach in taking the statements. If the record shifts from first person to second person to third person, two of the shifts should be replaced and only one, probably the third person point of view, should remain in the recorded version of the event.

Unlimited combined:

External observations mixed with personal ones combine to share points of view and often lend color or contrast to the reading when used expertly. The writer or editor knows when the use of a mixture of points of view is well use because the interactions are smooth and do not come across as contrived. Switches between people and places support the use of combined points of view but any change of who sees what or who says what must be controlled, reasonable, and easy to follow sequentially or risk losing the reader.

Natural shifts in perspective should occur and interest must be added to the thoughts presented. Readers are engaged and not aware of any transitions when actions flow naturally or logically. Otherwise, any bumps or disconnects are disconcerting.

One of the many advantages of a combined point of view is that it allows sharing of each character's thoughts of love, despair, longings and inner turmoil or other emotions. Knowing more about the inner thinking or attitudes of different characters adds riches to the entire reading or writing process.

Among the disadvantages of writing with a combined point of view is that the editing process is made far more complicated. The greater the number of significant people included in the overall plot, the greater the difficulty in writing and editing. Most of the challenge comes from assuring that each character is recognizable in varying locations and comes across as a uniquely separate person. The pleasure in reading is often sufficient to make up for the difficulties in preparation and presentation of multiple frenzies encountered in the multi-faceted views.

Narrator:

As an on-looker, a narrator can tell what is happening to whom, but cannot be inside a person's mind unless, of course, the person being described has the same intuitions or philosophical bent as the narrator. When editing and establishing a point of view, decide if an absent narrator is justified. A narrator's comments may be better presented as dialogue.

Both objective and subjective approaches can be used with a narrator's third person points of view. For example, a narrator can interject subjective opinions, or the opinions can come from a character. A *hidden* third-person *narrator* is often the writer, but it's complicated. When the author steps in, it may come across as disconcerting or as an intrusion and break up the flow of the story.

The voice outside the story may not be a character within the story itself. Flash-backs are one example where the use of a narrator can be helpful. Hans Christian Anderson was a master story-teller who was both in and outside of his stories. Simultaneously, he held accuracy paramount.

Other narrators may not describe a situation accurately, nor be reliable as observers. The narrator in William Faulkner's <u>The Sound and the Fury</u> is an example of living inside one's own head, and shifting points of view to exploit psychological decay. Unless a writer shows a narrator as mentally unstable, whether intoxicated, dim-witted, or mentally imbalanced, readers ordinarily assume the narrator to be dependable in all the descriptions included.

An edit should assure that readers discern the level of reliability of a narrator that is intended by the writer. If a narrator comes across as dependable in the early part of the story and later is portrayed as duplicitous, the change become part of the plot and, therefore, should be made clear. If not made clear during editing or revisions, readers may or may not know why they find the writing incomplete or even unsatisfying.

How a point of view is used is more important that which kind of voice is chosen. Changes from one point of view or voice (first, second, or third, etc.) depend largely on experience and skill. Erroneous shifts happen. When a writer unintentionally changes from the first person to the second person, the error should be corrected during editing.

An editor can be an excellent critic or may skip over sloppy work and ignore words that need to be changed. A writer also can edit and be especially diligent to find or make changes that need to be made in any point of view chosen. Sections where strong interactions of different voices are mixed with non-pertinent information should be carefully scrutinized. Edits shorten some sections, the point of view may need to be changed or adapted, or more dialogue may need to be included rather than have long sections of narratives.

Removal of unnecessary words, irrelevant asides, awkward or unclear phrasing and other obstacles must be caught and 'repaired.' But (there is always a 'but') how sure can an early edit recognize that what seems 'unnecessary' is actually a critical piece of a puzzle that will only be revealed later?

Writers who want to include different points of view may learn from analyzing the work of well-published authors. Skilled editors also benefit by attempts to edit established works of fiction. Any person who shifts from being a writer to becoming an editor of their own work benefits from the analysis and subsequently revisions of the points of view used. Multiple suggestions for possible changes do not imply negative criticisms. Suggestions made during editing refer only to the work at hand and do not imply any personal criticism.

CHAPTER THREE

Plots And Themes

"We are entangled in the outcome of what we do; we have to stand its consequences."

- John Dewey

The experiences, style, or attitudes of the writer may be the only distractions that deter the story from being well told. The story itself can justify the efforts needed to continue, but the writer need not continue the journey without help.

Focus:

Whatever focus taken during the writing process, it can be enhanced during the editing process. Scenes promote characters, plots, or themes which are justifications for universal motives. Arrangement of the scenes can promote action, gather suspense, move emotions, or simply get in the way of understanding what is happening.

To determine where the focus is within a scene, the elements of interaction between characters and the setting descriptions can be stripped out and examined. What will then stand out are any fallacies, contradictions, or any social commentary that interferes with action or progression of the story. Understanding of what the underlying theme is may also surface.

If the focus of a work is on the characters who must carry the story, verbal interactions are a necessity. Crisp, clear, personal biases, human weaknesses, and individual levity or hates must come across. A focus on the plot emphasizes inner motives, decisions, traumas, uncertainties, emotional and mental attitudes. Various kinds of mental or imaginative wanderings can heighten suspend is a scene or become absurd ramblings that come across as stream-of-consciousness writing.

Nonsensical and disconnected sentences add to images of characters trying to speak while in a drunken stupor, but in general such ramblings must be limited. The approach of exaggeration may work well in select areas, but edit out excessive meanderings and tighten the focus. Polish, refine, and tighten whenever possible. Listen to edit suggestions. If the focus is missing or if a section or scene is not necessary, cut it.

Fickle or wishy-washy writing styles promote disconcerting writing or may lead to interesting diversions. It is simple enough to say that good writing should flow. It is not simple for any writer to find a style that promotes good writing. It is critical that each writer/editor know how to identify styles that consistently flow without being fickle and disconcerting to readers. A case in point is suspense/thriller writer Johnathan Kellerman who had 40 books published between 1980 and 2009. The style and approach adopted by Kellerman sets a modern tone yet adheres to the age-old standard of quality reading.

Well accepted by editors, publishers, and the reader public, Kellerman's style relies mostly on one or two sentences per paragraph. Occasionally, a paragraph stretches to three sentences or more. Only when he includes descriptions of various settings does Kellerman resort to semi-long paragraphs. His short, choppy sentences promote quick and interesting reads without major gaps.

Humanizing inanimate objects lends flavor to what could be slow-downs to action. "A ring-in buzzer was topped by a tarnished bronze sign so small it seemed intent on avoiding discovery." (The Clinic, Ballentine Books, N. Y., 1977, p. 80). Divergence from traditional literary rules have prompted new approaches and new levels of interest in ingenuity.

Brevity is emphasized by many current writers regardless of the total length of the work attempted. Patterns can emerge that ignore standard punctuation rules and produce lively substance even if it appears in abbreviated form.

In writing, as in editing, creative thinkers can be the best critics. Some follow all of the rules. Others make up rules as they go forward with wayward approaches taken to surprise various audiences. Standard principles have value as stern guides for the mechanics of writing and for the complexities of editing. Principles need not be rigid, however, to support contemporary concepts in writing or those applied to editing.

Principles of editing are much like those of story-telling in that some kind of order must be imposed over the natural chaos that describes human behaviors. Editing demands that all of the pieces of a work be recognized, put into an appropriate place, and a whole created out of multiple seemingly disparate parts.

Contrived language that has no purpose is usually recognized. Jousting with invented words and linguistic gymnastics can be ignored or the process of editing can change the most convoluted sentences into powerful descriptions or dialogues. Control of what is left – or added—can filter out intrusive asides and strengthen the story. Extraneous information can be cut or changed only if it is recognized for what it is: unnecessary. Egotistical wishes on the part of a writer are no substitute for thorough examinations and critical objectivity. Pretentious wording and melodramatic descriptions need to be cut or changed. Each word can be shaped and each section crafted in much the same way that rough two-by-fours are discarded when the intent is to choose wood appropriate to the finish of a fine cabinet. Rough inappropriate words won't escape the scrutiny of a skilled editing review.

A plot is a plan that includes a direction and a result. Circling around every journey are other fragments that lead into variations of quests, intents, outcomes or messages. Variations in stories and their emphases abound. There are thousands of plot variations, but only one plot remains throughout all mystery, suspense, romance, science fiction, fantasy, or autobiographical fiction.

Each book is a puzzle cut from multiple pieces, some scattered, others dropped off the table, while some pieces lay neglected turned face down, left unused. A mystery of sorts, each story is a challenge waiting to be formed with multiple beginnings or different endings, to be put together with diligence and patience. *Who* and *What* carry the plot. *Where*, *When*, and *Why* hold the plot together.

The pieces fit together or they warp the progression from one event to the next.

Aristotle described six elements of writing, interpreted as character, thought, diction, lyrical poetry, and spectacle. Through the decades, these six elements have changed little. The way characters thought, their diction, and the spectacles writers conceived still make vibrant stories. Lyrical poetry has changed styles many times and novelists may include short or lengthy lyrical passages in works that are otherwise suspense, romance, or other relatively straightforward fiction.

Story line:

A story line follows the leading character's goal, usually to solve some form of crisis and come out victoriously over each obstacle encountered throughout the entire narrative. Getting a leading character into and out of bad situations equates to fine story-telling. But continually harping on disappointments, struggles, dangers, confrontations that include mental and/or physical hardships, all become tiresome without an editor's keen eye. Astute editing contributes to demonstrating a hero's win over adversity and finally reaching a goal set forward in the story line, the plot, and the theme.

Well constructed plots have both characters and location introduced at the beginning. Readers want to know the people involved and where they are. Why they are there may be able to wait until later as long as readers know a main character is at a particular location. For example:

"Charlotte knew the blood on her face and the blurs of tall buildings she passed made no sense, but she kept walking. Soon, she told herself. Soon she would be back at work,

looking at familiar objects, hearing multiple voices answer different phones. Where was the building? I'll be there soon. Yes, soon. I have to keep walking."

Charlotte is hurt and confused. She is in a city. She thinks she knows where her office is, but is unsure. Suspense builds but the introductions of person and place are made and the story begins.

Suspense novels, straight detective stories, and mysteries include some types of danger, accidents, perils, and even murder. Other plots include similar difficulties explained in various scenes and challenges are overcome when the entire plot comes together. Major characters, occasional guests, family members, and acquaintances or distant strangers make up the cast of the story as it evolves. All of the significant players need not be introduced early in the story since some are not important until the plot progresses and their introductions make sense.

The main story line deserves more space than the diversions even when some of the asides may be full subplots. A tight story line allows the lead character to live through one bad situation at a time while continuing to face difficulties. Loose story lines meander from back story through durations of side events and personality quirks. A solid edit can detect when too many distractions throw the entire effort askew.

Chronologically based stories are more easily followed both in writing and in reading. *Now* is a point in time most readers can identify as being critical. *Later* may not be important, but it can raise speculation as to what can happen. A point in time when something takes place or is about to take place must be clearly shown. Lack of information about when something takes place causes confusion and mixing up time sequence can distract the reader who has to go back to see if something was missed.

Editing for omissions in time sequences takes a high level of focus. Disparities in time sequences can easily be checked and should be corrected during the revision or editing process, otherwise sections may be skipped intentionally by the reader. Chronological time must be kept logical, but time factors are not the only stumbling points. How various characters got to certain places or when they got to some place or the other must be both accurate and reasonable unless the intention is to leave blanks that must be filled in by readers' imaginations.

Descriptions need to be accurate. Real places need to be described as they exist within the story. When an old story is being told, an old map can be useful to both writer and editor. If streets no longer exist, or some of the street names have been changed, a new map may be needed by both writer and editor. Disclaimers often suffice for made-up places and imagined streets, but when an actual city is used as part of the plot, don't let the chase end up in the river unintentionally. Either keep places real, or be sure that fictional places remain fictional.

Types of plots:

During the twentieth and at the beginning of the twenty-first centuries, six kinds of plots became widely recognized: *Person against Self; Person against Person; Person against Nature; Person* against *Society; Person against Machine; Person against a deity.* Regardless of the variety and the vast differences among all of the details, universally, there is only one plot: *a journey.*

Person against Self stories usually take an internal observation approach in which internal existence of psychological demons are faced, or not, in narratives and dialogues. Individual or universal in nature, the theme of struggle and adversities encountered and overcome against all probability of success can be poignant or simply distressing. Continually presenting only one person's point of view can be limiting to the plot envisioned. Edits to expand beyond first person hurdles can be valuable. Different types of stories need different approaches and many find the use of third person point of view easier to write, to read, and to edit than first person manuscripts.

Herman Melville's *Moby Dick* includes *Person against Person* aggressions but the main conflict of the novel is *Person against Nature* because of Ahab's obsession to destroy the white whale he thought of as 'Moby Dick.'

Person against Person and *Person against Society* manuscripts usually fall into the suspense, detective, or mystery categories. A good edit may determine whether or not conflicts escalate, or if the suspense factor becomes the rapid heartbeat of the tale being told. When suspense is too drawn out, some deletions may be in order, or some re-arranging of different pieces may be beneficial.

Detective stories usually require more puzzle-solving than either mysteries or straight suspense stories. That does not mean that there should not be an emotionally laden story. The emphasis shifts, but all other elements can be included, even a bit of romance as appropriate. Whatever the emphasis, authenticity is important and all the conflicts and situations included must be believable as well as the outcomes. Even superheroes and their antics must come across to readers as if anything is possible.

Editing a mystery involves recognition of situational and emotional conflicts that lead to, or result from, some kind of trauma, including murder. It is easier to introduce characters early in the story and show why they are involved emotionally in whatever trauma besets them and why they have the potential to succeed in their journey.

Early introductions help speed readers toward acceptance of the characters and the anticipated plot, and the involvement of the reader creates interest in how the future of the plot can unfold. Particular problems can be introduced that can lead to future fatalities or deeper traumas to be overcome or absolved as the story gains momentum.

If the writer is unfamiliar with some details usually accepted as a part of police procedures such as crime scene tactics, or other technical or legal protocols, research needed both by the writer and editor can clarify whatever is included. Reliable sources are available and good writers use them to enhance specific or obscure data. Editors also use outside sources to research particular information when the veracity of statements or actions are unclear. Including accuracy imbedded in the details of plots or sub-plots increases readability and appreciation from possible audiences

Crime writers know there are terms that should be precise for each category of victims used. For example, when young people voluntarily leave home they are described as 'runaways.' Infants, children, or youths who are abandoned or thrown out of their home are referred to as 'throw-aways.' 'Stolen' children are abducted by strangers or relatives (for profit or abuse) and are most often 'snatched' or 'kidnapped' and their disappearances are examined by the Federal Bureau of Investigation (FBI). 'Family victims' describes those of every age who suffer abuse from family members. Knowing and using precise terms and accurate descriptions are the responsibility of both writers and editors.

Plots that focus on *Person against Nature, Person against Machine,* or *Person against a diety* demand specific details. Botany, physiology, geography, geology, or weather systems analysis along with other scientific information may be needed to fully develop a *Person against Nature* theme and explain all of the concomitant dangers that become obstacles. Skills of various characters need to be described when nefarious ways generally outside of common knowledge are included.

Underwater exploration equipment or techniques along with mapping expertise or knowledge of support gear may have to be researched if a *Person against Nature* plot involves escapades such as searching for lost underwater treasures. Ocean, lake or river scenes may have to include information on water pressures, depth details and various perils. When accurate, different scenes may be sketchy but acceptable to readers when small details seem valid. Unusual geographically physical conditions or plants and medicines found in obscure places enrich nature struggles but can be damaging to the entire story when errors are not caught in the editing process.

Stories of *Person against Machine* abound. Computers, space ships able to transport, telephonic invasions, others conceived imaginatively or scientifically construed usually require verification of factual statements included. Science fiction allows more freedom from research by its definition, but usually involves some verification of feasibility.

Person against a diety theme and subsequent plots require either understanding of various nuances of spiritual struggles or extensive research on theological matters, or both. Other factors may well need to be researched to round out any specifics of whatever century or location is chosen. Various traditions, archaic customs, primordial or prehistoric events may help identify dangers encountered by various characters as the plot expands.

Creeds, dogmas, doctrines and teleological differences abound. Theological terms are particular to different locations, religions, and even languages. Many readers, writers and editors may know what words such as *basilica, chantry,* or *nave* mean. They may not know what *pyx, apse,* or *oriel* mean. A *pyx* is the box in which wafers consecrated for the Eucharist ceremonies are kept. An *apse* is the same as *apsis*, a semicircular or polygonal projection of a building, especially from the east side of a domed church. Whenever there is no explanation of what a word means, an edit can help add clarity.

Adding an off-hand explanation by a character usually works when some dictionary help is needed.

Organization:

Some editors simply read and decide that they can support the plot as presented. Other editors want to know what needs to change when a plot is not really a plot or why it seems to be so. Many editors know when the plot doesn't work as well as they'd like but they are uncertain as to how it can be fixed.

Rarely does a writer look at the total organization of the work and some writers focus only on a small portion that seems out of place. Generally, it all comes down to whether or not the overall efforts convey a sense of reality even when the story is science fiction and is intended to be beyond imaginary. In other words, the story must be valid, or at least perceived to be possible.

One measure of validity is that all events follow in some logical order, unless a well-explained back-story or a future imaging is interjected. All events, real or imagined, should be related to or caused by all preceding events. Simply put, there is a time sequence and a cause and effect relation to all action in every plot. Every act has a reason and every consequence is identified. When the plot wobbles between capricious acts with no motive and no consequences, an editor looks hard at basic integration of the material even when the writing sparkles and the action is tingling.

Convoluted material often is easier to edit when the sections are thought of as three big blocks. Each block has a beginning, middle, and an end. Each section has dynamic scenes and interesting people who carry the action to different places and readers understand why events unfold a particular way. Edits proceed more easily when the entire process is manageable and separate sections are examined for different reasons.

The plot is structured much like the Bell Curve. The *beginning* is about one-fourth of the total length of whatever type of fiction is attempted. The *middle* is usually about one-half of the total length of the work. The *end* includes the final one-forth of the total work. Plot is a problem or problems presented and decisions made or the directions taken toward finding solutions to any challenges encountered and to solving every problem.

The Beginning:
Introductions are important. The beginnings of every adventure capture the imagination and hold the audience captive through knowing who, on a first-hand basis, will be the focus of the actions to come and showing

something about what kind of fretful actions will follow. All the important elements of the story are introduced within the first one-third of the total work.

The lead character must be dominant in whatever crisis prompts the setting of the story and in whatever type plot is chosen. No matter who other major players in the story may be, other characters must either be sympathetic with, or be in opposition to, the hero character. Personalities of significant characters should be clearly distinctive and portrayed as either supportive or as adversarial.

Settings are important because readers want to know where the people they share time with went and why they went where they did. The different places in which action takes place are explained either briefly or in great detail. When places are described too completely excessive details such as how a plant survives in the high desert become a distraction. Alert editing helps keep the balance between *who* and *where*.

Writers may not go back and check to see if the introductions made for each person are strong enough to be remembered later in the story, but editors do. When key people are introduced and it is established where they are and why they are there, the plot is supported. Distinctive introductions of people reinforce the story line and help set a pace for all that follows. What they are doing in a particular place at a specific time is helpful to the reader's understanding and expectations of what is to follow.

A review edit assures that a beginning section does what it is supposed to do in the way of introductions of lead characters and primary locations. *Who* and *where* and *why* questions are answered even when locations change and when various actions complete the story.

The Middle:

Life and daily activities are filled with surprises but writers and editors try to avoid unexplained events and keep confusion to a bare minimum. Fiction readers thrive on surprise and fiction writers employ surprises as liberally as is practical. Fiction writer/editors check through the pages regularly to see if enough surprise elements are included, if some would be better re-located, or if some should be left out.

Just as visual artists allows the eye to rest within a fine painting or design, the best writers allow the reader to catch a breath by allowing an occasional pause or gap between fast action followed too closely with one surprise after another. Extra words do not always contribute to the overall impact of any section and tight stories are usually more interesting.

The lead character should face higher and higher stakes in an effort to reach whatever goal is ahead. Failures, or obstructions to reaching a goal, should become more complex and perhaps more frequent as the story gets more and more complicated. Struggles to move though or avoid obstacles put into the path of the lead character puts life into the story. The pain or disappointments felt by the lead character(s) show real people moving through real events to resolve conflicts and crises that created their need to reach a goal in the first place.

About halfway through the middle of a work of fiction, there usually is a BIG surprise that heightens interest and heightens action. The unexpected surprise helps keep the plot from dragging and helps keep the reader guessing. If placement and appropriateness of the surprise is effective and the end result of including the surprise helps the dramatics at the correct point in the story, then it usually has a good result. If the placement is questionable, some changes are indicated.

When the surprise is effective, the lead character may go in circles, on tangents, or meet dead ends as the quest to overcome obstacles proceeds to enhance the story. Some of the peripheral characters may disappear or be explained away at this point, but the reader must not be confused as to why they were included in the first place.

Regardless of how many people are encountered along the way, the lead character should always be more important than anyone else in the story. Occasionally, a belligerent character will take over the story and slide into the hero's job. Upstaged, the hero depends on the editor to re-do the upstart's efforts and assure that each plot and sub-plot moves emphasis back where it belongs: on the main story character and on the main story line.

Toward the end of the middle, another BIG surprise helps heighten the intensity of the plot. The last surprise of the middle can be an obstacle, a failure, a dead end, recognition that the approach taken by the hero was all wrong, or a heightened awareness of something of importance that has surfaced and become attached to the original goal.

Along the way, the writer/editor must assure that the lead character comes across as likeable. It is immaterial that the lead may be a criminal, be a really bad person, or just plain loco. Whether evil or filled with goodness, the lead must have personal characteristics that create empathy in the reader, and displays whatever it takes in the way of personal intent or physical stamina to demonstrate courage in the face of every danger.

The End:

Actions, reactions, and connected events tell the story. Ways in which the theme, plots, sub-plots and all of the separate components of each are tied together and stacked against each other determine how and what the end will be and establish the outcome.

Every component included plus any significant event that happens in the opening, in the middle, and in the end, all lead to the climax. As the end progresses, the lead character encounters fewer and fewer choices about how to reach the original goal. Beginning with lesser characters, wrap up any unanswered issues such as "What happened to Joe?"

A thorough review with corrections can resolve matters that create confusion or at least take out elements that may not relate to the flow of the plot. Editing helps assure that the lead character's goals are met, any dilemmas overcome, and that there are achievements at the end. All loosely drawn conclusions are clarified and the end is satisfying.

If a writer begins a story at the beginning and finds that the ending is elusive, one approach is to start at the end and work backwards to reach a beginning. Another approach is to let the end flow naturally from the beginning. Tarantino films purposely start stories at the end and work backwards. This approach takes extreme planning and is difficult for beginning writers but has its own appeal to readers and to editors since the end is clear from the beginning, or at least potentially so.

Some writers make extensive outlines which become useful tools for the editor and subsequent guides when examining questions about logical order of events or scenes. An entire novel can be reduced to an intensely scrutinized legal-sized page before any writing begins when a writer/editor needs to see if the entire approach with its various twists and tangles is sound. When a weak ending appears, it is easier to throw away part of an outlined single page than it is to throw away weeks or months of written words.

Themes:

Themes, plots, and sub-plots and their components are interrelated yet separate packages by which a story is told. Occasionally, a theme can be described in a simple sentence and tells what the story is supposed to be about. Some describe themes as the tone or even a setting that frames the work, but the true theme is the underlying message or intent. A theme unfolds as the story unfolds. The writer decides what (if any) messages are important. The editor helps decide what messages are conveyed or if any need to be changed, emphasized, or deleted.

Themes can include different emphases. Examples of themes include: escape, revenge, riddles, quest, rescue, rivalry, pursuit, temptation, transformation, love, metamorphosis, discovery, sacrifice, success, failure, entertainment, skill development, anxiety, mental breaks, or as many as the writer wants to include. The editor may help judge if the theme or the multiple themes included are necessary.

Themes run through and across plots and set the level of excitement (if any) that illustrate each subplot within the main story. The message that a writer intends to convey can come across from the theme or thread that runs through the final work. If the writer intends to entertain, the work reflects that intention either subtly or openly. Having a single purpose does not deter the writer from following an informative theme interspersed through an entertainment theme or from using any combination of themes or sub-themes al long as they do not become too confusing.

Sub-themes may enrich an approach or they may confuse the outcome. The pace and tone of the story sets the theme in motion and can enhance the purpose of letting the underlying theme be known to readers. Knowing the purpose(s) of a work is a technique to guide the process of developing the work and a clear purpose helps evaluate the work during the polishing and editing phases.

Readers may not be interested in the techniques used by a writer/editor when a story captures their minds and/or their emotions. Writers may go forward with whatever theme captures their own imagination regardless of who the audiences may be. Editors try to keep their own imaginations outside the story in order to see if the writing holds to its intentions and is technically accurate according to its purpose. An editor's suggestions may require revising the plot, the story line, or the theme. Accomplishing such work is less than awe inspiring, but each adjustment is well worth the time and effort required when a story needs to be improved.

Parallel Themes:

Parallel themes, or story lines that run along with the major plot, can be an interesting approach for both the writer and the reader. Parallel themes, sometimes called sub-themes, can be an important part of the major plot and can be equally compelling to readers. Parallel themes often include a separate set of main characters and their actions which complement the main plot. When separate sets of characters are used, the editing process should assure the separation occurs without distracting the reader and without confusing the main story. One example of parallel themes is the television series "Downton Abbey" where the gentry and household staff are separate but complementary to the plot and sub-plots.

Also, the British television series "Upstairs Downstairs" masterfully presents parallel themes when the lives of the gentry are in contrast with those of the serving classes. The complementary and oppositions of the classes help define the differences between the various groups involved in the story. Reader and viewer involvement is complete when each parallel theme highlights individual characters and the toils of each life are portrayed sufficiently.

To determine the suitability of parallel themes and where they appear in the work is an editing challenge. If a parallel theme puts an unexpected event in chapter one when it could strengthen the story and perhaps heighten suspense if it were placed in a later chapter or expanded or even deleted if not saved until later, a decision has to be made. Examination of the placement of different sections is often ignored, but well worth the effort to change where a section belongs if clarity is the goal.

Sub-themes:

Sub-themes may reflect back to some earlier point in time or they may be used to project action into the future, and there can be more than one sub-theme provided each enhances the overall story. Sub-themes let the reader move among different events or different characters in different places, or at different times, without leading the reader into confusion. Sub-themes are asides, but not distractions, and should add to the major story line rather than be simple diversions.

Used skillfully, sub-themes help avoid monotony. Sub-themes (or sub-plots) can be written as parallel tracks when the action takes place at the same time. They can be presented as parallels to reflect what different people are doing at the same time or in a closely related place. When people are in different places, or doing something at different times, sub-themes add to a story as long as the activities or thoughts reflected by the different people converge at some point.

Some questions asked in review of placements of sub-plots include: 'Why is this happening now? Why can't this be clearer if it takes place later?' There may be more or better questions, but when there is no reason for a particular sub-plot to be part of a particular section or even an entire work, change it or edit it out.

Writer/editor's objectivity helps determine when the sub-themes become too complex or too tangled to support clear and intriguing writing. *Moby Dick* is an example of interesting rambling sub-plots that support the vagaries of Melville's works. Melville's writing is internationally known, reviewed by experts, and critically acclaimed. Many story tellers of great fame ramble and include diversions that are not always necessary to solid story telling. William Faulkner, for example, is touted by some scholars as a masterful story teller. Others find Faulkner twisted and otherwise maudlin when many asides of self pity make his work convoluted and unappealing.

Readers vary in reaction to different writers. Editors try to keep reader audiences in mind when balancing recommendations on ways to improve the story's presentation and entice reader involvements. When writers seek and find their own originality, success as an author can be expected.

Lietmotief:

Some writers use the musical approach and have a dominant theme as the work moves from heavy tension to quiet respite. Too much loud music can prompt deafness. Too many soft musical or written reflections can put readers to sleep. A work can be made more interesting when the intent is kept but the emotional impact is varied. As in music, the reader audience must be allowed to have a respite after much intensity that is sustained too long. In other words, keep the intent, but vary the emotional impact. Let the reader catch a breath.

High intensity of emotions and relentless struggles of main characters can become exhausting to readers. Plots which are high-wire circus acts should include safety nets which allow for subtler swings and gentler actions on the part of the characters. Edits can space out the drum-rolls and reader reactions by adding landscape descriptions, physical movements, attitudes, and other diversions much like a gentle rain to diffuse high intensity.

Examinations of the way in which the work is put together are primary tasks of editing. Starting with plot or story, one editing task will be to determine if the story adequately supports the characters and if the characters carry the plot to a logical outcome. The structure critique is major and difficult although an objective overview easily gets diverted when the plot is interesting and the characters are compelling. Emotional involvements in the story are put aside less distractions interfere with good editing.

Most plots run throughout a work in chronological order. Some plots use back stories or time lapses or even future imaginings. Regardless of the technique or style chosen, the story starts at a specific place and time. Modern works are influenced by the rapid pace of videos, movies, computer games, etc. thus they mimic fast pace and rapid action sequences. Regardless of the pace, the plot may cover hours, days, months, years, decades, or multi-generations yet still focus on one main character's journey in a logical time sequence.

Flash-backs or back stories should remain true to the intent of the theme and should move toward a believable conclusion. Editing should examine the underlying solidity of the work as it is constructed and as it moves forward. Flash-backs may be put in an awkward place, or if the story becomes confused because of flash-backs, they may be put in different chapters to improve clarity.

Writers can review their work to see if flashbacks interfere with understanding. When one person tells another about what happened years ago, it probably seems natural. When a full-blown flash-back is inserted, it may be distracting and crowd the plot. An editor can look at the balance between crowding in too much or including too little to allow the story to progress.

Balance within the structure becomes a benchmark for both writer and editor. Examine the story as it unfolds. During the polishing process, look for structural gaps as well as overly wordy phrases and excessive descriptions. Wanderings seldom add much, but often distract readers and tempt them to put the works down. Whenever possible, shorten phrases and deleted overly pompous words to tighten action and keep the reader engaged.

Comical writing:

Conventional exaggerations can shift from trite repetitions to fresh translation of sparkling comedy. Quirky personalities that trail in and out of the plot can help add interest, but also can be unreliable to the story. If too much dark humor follows one character, or there is too much internal turmoil that seems out of place, an edit may turn a morbid scene into an absurdly funny situation.

Surprise portrayals apply to settings but may also reflect characters involved in the same or in different settings. Some add comic relief such as when the famous star Carol Burnett, dressed in a ragged floor-scrubber's outfit, pretends she's on stage as a high class stripper. Burnett's garb puts her out of sync with sexy motions. The opposite of what is usual makes the scene funny because it is unexpected.

Comic writing doesn't please everyone, nor does it make everyone laugh. Often, comedy misses the audience's interest and fails to amuse. Comic interjections into action writing, however, may endear a character or provide respites to tense action or trauma scenes. Even monks can be made jolly or mischievous to add flavor to their usual strict or humorless lives.

In general, mystery stories don't lend themselves to comedy. Murder or spy stories are usually tense and action filled. A few funny characters can lend some relief to the intensity of action, or one person can fill the role of comic because they have a funny streak added as part of their personality. Without prospects of their antisocial dispositions being redeemed, murderers and traitors can spark positive responses if touched by a sense of the ridiculous.

Comic reactions may be interjected by sarcastic irony or be included as plain silliness. The editing process determines how much silly business is enough. If each scene is too exaggerated to be effective, the scene may need to be omitted or at least shortened to keep comic reactions valid. Caution is advised. If an external editor has a different sense of humor than the writer, sarcasm or irony may be missed altogether. External advice on changes should always be heeded even when different approaches are suggested. A small change may be all it takes to turn dry sarcasm into funny relief.

Too many surprises lose their effectiveness. While one surprise is comical, too many become tiresome. Repetitions can lead to dullness and show amateurism but can be edited out if they are recognized. Simple shortening may make a big difference in whether or not a scene is effective or dull.

Punch lines either enhance or destroy pace or plot when they are intended to be funny but fall short. Clever lines, written so that the real personality of a character shows through, always benefit the story. When false acts or motives belie word choices, the story suffers. One editing approach is to decide to let comic asides stay in a scene or to forget trying to include funny quips and leave comic writing to acknowledged pros.

CHAPTER FOUR

Scenes And Settings

"The train was loaded to capacity, and the shrill notes of hysteria in the confusion of voices were the pleas for space in vestibules and aisles."

- Ayn Rand

The concept of scenes evolved from the theater where certain people (actors) are encapsulated in specific settings which display locations illustrated by back-drops, sound-tracts, and lighting. In written materials, locations combine with points in time to carry readers and a story's characters into and through plots and sub-plots. Scenes may be concentrated in one setting or they may span continents. Time factors may be limited or they may encompass decades or centuries.

In stage and screen productions, settings are backgrounds for action assisted by costumes, props, and special effects. In writing, settings are the locations where one or more people do something; where each scene takes place. Some settings are tranquil, placid, safe, commonplace, or places where quiet people carry out quiet lives. In contrast to the ordinary, exotic or darkly somber places call for mysteries and dangers. Unconventional settings tend to provide surprise or suspense.

Scenes may take place in hostile environments, richly elegant places, old dilapidated houses, beside quiet seascapes, on city streets, or in stuffy parlors. A ski lift implies more action than a back table at the local library. Settings, along with specific periods of time, provide shadow and light to characters and their behaviors.

Theater scenes are limited by space, availability of various technical or design crews, materials, acting talents, and money. With a bountiful supply of all that is needed to mount a full theater production, the result can be an extravaganza. Small or grandiose theatrical productions can be extremely effective when strong characters in dynamic or subtle settings explore consequences with dramatic effects. The same applies to written scenes.

The size of scenes or the details of settings become less than important when clear interactions between characters are paramount. Agatha Christie and Dorothy Sayers mastered the art of allowing characters to engage in enthralling events while limiting setting to various English drawing rooms or to British country villages.

Scenes are judged by readers with multiple experiences who have witnessed many kinds of scenarios. Written scenes are limited by a writer's imagination and attention to detail. Images float within a writer's mind, but it is difficult to be exact or poignant when visualized scenes are described in written verbiage.

Writer/editors may discover – or fail to see – the same image as intended. If the scene or setting is foggy, the editor's task is to guide the intended scene into clarity. To drop a phrase, tighten a sentence, or choose a different word becomes a challenge. In the process of clarifying, the writer/editor watches for stumbling clauses, inappropriate settings, and even such details as misplaced apostrophes.

Scenes in familiar locations create various moods. Moods can be projected by the locations or they can be demonstrated through the words or the acts of various characters. Details can startle, soothe, arouse emotions, or prompt nostalgia. Scenes which are used to highlight various moods, including hatred, animosity, laziness, resistance, personality quirks, or joyful bliss, may rely on distinctive settings. Settings may enhance the identity of characters and support their inclinations to act a certain way. Lovers don't always need to watch a sunset, nor do criminals always lurk in dark alleys.

Settings can be suitable or unsuitable to the basic physical appearance of people. Reasons why people are where they are either helps continue the storyline or there are gaps that need to be filled. When reasons are weak or confusing, something should get changed during editing.

The physical characteristics of people and their personalities should belong in the environs in which they are placed and in the appropriate time as described in much the same way sneakers and tuxedos are worn appropriately. A hobo who struts across the polished marble entry of a Wall Street bank won't ordinarily belong in such a place. Unless the disguise is that of the bank's president who wants to know how each customer is treated, a hobo in a bank lobby doesn't fit and the setting is askew or it is intentionally suspenseful.

Writers make choices and build on their own observations while editors point out missed opportunities to use settings as enhancements to scenes and plots. Scenes and the setting in which they take place can be simple or elaborate. Homely settings can be as powerful as elegant surroundings. The homely may be mixed with grandiose ones if some purpose in doing so is achieved. A mix may expand the understanding of a person and can enhance the story. During edits of various scenes, any mixtures of different places or different people should relate to the plot as a whole. Otherwise, there is confusion.

Action scenes often include mere sketches of surroundings and/or bare mention of specific places. Descriptions of various environments do not have to be long, but should be accurate without too many frills. A writer should know that a prickly pear does not define a specific location and could mean either South Carolina's coastal area or Utah's high desert. Adding a few specifics such as a long-armed Joshua tree narrows the location to the southwest of the United States but is not yet specific enough. There is usually no need to describe how the land became dotted with thorny plants, how various iguana survive, or that rattlesnakes like to hide in the shade near warm rocks. Brevity is acceptable as long as there is assurance that each scene is accurate and allows complete understanding of where the action takes place.

Unless the settings included have a purpose and move the plot forward, they should be shortened or cut completely. Descriptions of a plant, rocks, mountains or some other point of reference can be included in dialogue and talked about by the people involved. Brief mentions are usually enough to give flavor as to why or how something happens in a particular setting. Rain can divert action, or it can enhance danger. If it rains too often or for too long a period, change it. If rain contributes to ongoing struggles, leave it.

Changes in settings or scenes can further actions without allowing a break in tension and carefully crafted transitions can effectively lead into further action. Place or time changes shift readers from one perspective to another. A simple sentence or a sharp change in action may serve as a bridge from one state of activity to a different one. The type of changes can reflect shifts in emotions, in thoughts, decisions, or even attitudes taken by different characters.

In written materials, editors consider cliff hangers as tools used with caution. There are occasions when a cliff-hanger makes a good transition scene, but too many cliff-hangers become obvious and cheapen a writer's efforts. Popular in the l950's to entice movie-goers, virtually every movie theater included a chilling cliff-hanger that was continued the following week. The growing sophistication of all audiences caused the short mystery shows to be replaced with previews of coming attractions. Written materials followed when change of scene methods were used to replace the more obvious cliff hanger approach.

Scene openers can be teasers to set a mood for what follows or perhaps lead into new events. Openers also can be extenders of the scene previously included. To open a scene, play with words. Change the urgency, the mystery, the anger, the challenges, or some other facet of the scene to make the reader wonder what comes next or to add depth to the people in the story. Question the length, depth, or the necessity of adding or deleting some section but be sure the purpose of the scene supports the larger story and adds to the interest intended. Options for beginning a scene fall into categories that can be scrambled around to satisfy the writer and catch the imagination of the reader.

Elizabeth George, in her book <u>Write Away</u> (Harper Collins, N. Y. 2004, p. 70) calls the need to show the reader a "tool of craft." She lists eight tools. (Examples were selected by the author of <u>Editing—Ten Steps.)</u>

"1. Name a character in the book." (Herman Melville's *"Call me Ishmael"* – <u>Moby Dick.)</u>

"2. Tell the reader something significant in the plot." (Dickens, <u>Tale of Two Cities.)</u>

"3. Show a personality quirk...of one of the characters." (Poe's, *"The thousand injuries of Fortunado I had borne as best I could.')*

"4. Illustrate a character's attitude." (Faulkner's <u>Light in August</u>, *"But if you had more than mansense you would know that women don't mean anything when they talk. It's menfolks that take talking serious."*

"5. Show the way the narrator's mind works." (Morris West's <u>Proteus)</u> *"It's like a bloody conjuring trick. Now you see John Spada. Now he disappears in a puff of blue smoke! But I suppose the suckers will buy it."*

"6. Give a clue or thicken the plot or a foreshadowing of either." (Sidney Sheldon's <u>The Sands of Time)</u> *"The farmhouse memories came flooding back of the day the Morases had come to him after they had taken the little girl to the hospital."*

"7. Lead...into excitement." (A. E. Hotchner's <u>Papa Hemingway</u>, p.83.) *"I stood for a moment in the open doorway, shocked at his appearance."*

"8. Render a mysterious or suspenseful occurrence." (Robert Ludlum's <u>The Hades Factor)</u> *"Smith heard*

> *the voice as if from under miles of water at the bottom of a murky lagoon."*

Examples of ways to entice readers may come from a million different places. Hooks used in a developing work of fiction depend on a writer's background and preferences. An editor's task is to help keep the story moving and enticing regardless of the type of 'hook' used.

It is not up to the editor alone to add punch and excitement to a writer's story. Scenes can distract from the plot, don't engage the reader, or may be in the wrong place. Some scenes are so short they don't include enough information as to what's going on and, therefore, lack energy. Other scenes are short because they need to be short. Adding extras may stifle the intensity of a short scene.

Excessive information can defeat the purpose of a scene. Too many sex scenes with too many details can be unfavorable to otherwise likeable characters. Distaste on the part of readers can set in if a sex scene, or a fight scene, or a chase scene, go on and on with too many minor or drawn out details. Check the purpose of leaving long specialized scenes in place. When a scene is needed, leave it or shorten it. Short scenes usually are best at keeping reader interest.

How long should a scene be? A scene should be as long as it takes to include all the parts necessary to support the story. If the point of the scene gets muddled by too much detail, or includes more distractions than needed, it is too long. If the purpose of the scene is to convey some hidden message, or to better explain why a character behaves a certain way, enough detail should be included to make the meaning clear.

Edits help even experienced writers avoid too many mundane flourishes when adding touches or abbreviated notions to create a lasting impression of people or place not completely described. Readers are no more likely to recall "a tall girl watched scattered foam roll under the dark shadows of the encrusted piers" than they are "a sturdy pier hung over the dark ocean as she watched," or "it was dark on the pier where she sat." As presented here, each description is an incomplete scene, but each has a core. Each gives a sense of time and place plus the hint of a person. What is missing is conflict and duration of action. Resolution of whatever dilemma is taking place can be included or left to the next scene.

Flips or switches in action can occur in two different places with the same characters acting the way they usually do. Or, action can flip to people behaving differently in the same place. They may behave differently because their attitude, perceptions, or some new or outside information was received. When new elements come into a scene, it is both the writer's and the editor's job to make sure that some reason or explanation is given.

Switches from one place to another may increase suspense. Or, a change may relieve tension. A scene with the peril of a CEO in the midst of a frenzied stock market can switch to the quiet determination of a fraud examiner who does his best thinking while fishing.

Settings:

Readers should not have to wonder "Is this a contemporary place? Are these people in some future century? If this is medieval Europe, where are the dark alleys?" Good writers will not allow their readers to get lost. At least not for long. Settings can change with the actions but they are always specific to the story and do not leave the reader wondering where in the world the characters are, or have gone.

Settings may be one of the most overlooked tools a writer has available. Settings can influence action either negatively or they can move the action along. The settings can be too much alike or too repetitive. They may be too ordinary, or they can focus too much on a rug and not enough on some mysterious stain that forces future actions.

A place can be symbolic of a large belief system that can influence thoughts of the characters and their behaviors, or be an understructure of the plot if the place influences the belief system that destroys or builds the plot to support the story line. But, if the place is counter to the story and undermines the action, the writer has an obligation to change the location or to revise the actions that are prompted by the location.

If the story's main location is an inner-city building, the editing question may be why the lead character fell off a mountain. Use locations as incentives for actions that have explanations and include motives and do not let readers question how an activity took place somewhere that makes no sense in the sequences expected.

If accurately described, settings can be powerful. Since writers do not know who the readers are, accurate descriptions of locations are assets. Described wrongly, readers often become irritated. It is disconcerting to a reader or editor who knows a place well to find a description of a city and its various streets that is wrong. Whenever a real place is included, it deserves to be accurately described. Imaginary places have fictitious street names and wander in strange directions but even false streets in non-existing places must remain consistent throughout the stories in which they appear.

Most inaccuracies in settings are related to geography or historical facts. It matters when the setting takes place in Boston, Memphis, Albuquerque, Singapore, or in the Everglades, that each location is described with accuracy. A writer can be a good student of the place and actually spend some time on location, or stay at home and use Google, or find a good travel guide to use as a reference. When in doubt about a road that goes south or east, check it out. If a writer does not know which streets run in which direction, a map is useful. To invent locations and provide directions is silly when only the imagination is used to describe a real place. A particular setting must be important to a scene and descriptions should be compellingly vivid. Settings support a scene as a whole or can fragment the intent of the plot and become a disruption to the story. Rain storms affect actions and determine outcomes. Mention of the rain may be brief, or ramble on, but it must have meaning and carry the story forward. Without a purpose for being included, a particular setting or an entire scene may come across as contrived and unnecessary. Both are good reasons to eliminate either the setting or the whole scene.

Brief, extended, vague, or specific settings can affect and support either the major or the minor plot or they may influence characters in different ways. Descriptions of specific locations can enhance or distract a character's actions and take away from the main purpose of the scene. People should be in places where they belong within the story. A dock worker in oily clothes placed in a fancy tea parlor must have a reason for being there.

The writer/editor's job is to assure that each setting is appropriate to the story and is accurately and believably described. Each part of each setting must be where it belongs even in science fiction or fantasy. Wild daisies may grow between the cracks of city sidewalks in the slums, but they grow more believably on mountainsides. Blue spruce trees thrive in rugged cold areas but are seldom found on the dry plains of west Texas.

Different places smell and sound differently. A rural setting can have the silence of fog rising from a river or smell like freshly mowed hay. A remote farm can have domestic animal sounds and smells. New Orleans and San Francisco have large shipping ports with distinctive sounds and smells that are uniquely their own. Different areas have their own cultures, unique and specific types of storage or living conditions. Editors and readers discern falsehoods and invented descriptions. Weather, flora, terrain, and fauna require accurate descriptions.

Casinos fronting the Great Mississippi did not exist at the turn of the twentieth century, and more recently several were swept away during the great hurricane Katrina. Each era requires its own historical and geographical descriptors. The time and place of each setting must reflect that a specific place existed or even that a specific thing can happen there. When a writer does not know that palm trees do not grow in northern Canada, or that vivacious bougainvillea loves heat but dies in severe cold, the writing becomes suspect. By the same measure, when an editor does not catch such errors, the process of editing is suspect.

A setting, important and consistent, or limited and minor, reflects the surroundings of any profession included in the scene. Every field of expertise has its expected locations and many are unique. Oceanographers need oceans as much as train stories need central hubs for switching cargoes carried by rail. Physicians are identified with hospitals. Large lawyers firms are expected in large cities rather than in highly isolated areas.

The connections of profession to place are obvious although the settings used do not always support the idea of putting people and place together. Edit out contradictions to simplify the story and avoid any confusion created by illogical settings. Specific settings may imply more than the place where people live or where they work. Placing people in certain environments can support motives that underpin whatever actions are taken.

When a place is important to the plot, is an influence on the characters or to the action of the story, the setting becomes prominent. Even indoor settings reflect weather and geography. Personalities of characters can be shown by what is included in living spaces, by specific objects scattered around or carefully placed in an apartment or house. Architectural details can convey a sense of wealth or show only rustic decay. Scenes can be elegant or tawdry. Wherever they are, they reflect personalities, attitudes, and even tendencies to overcome difficulties or to succumb to adversities.

An excerpt from "*The Doctor*" by Franke is one example of ironic description.

"The doctor's office was crowded with shabby chairs. Dark brown slashes on the walls were perhaps intended to provide interest to otherwise colorless walls. Instead of being interesting, the slashes looked like bug leavings.

"I was tired. My leg hurt. Thank God it wasn't bleeding. I had fallen when the idiot kid from downstairs almost shot me. He was playing with the gun his step-father left out during a drunken stupor. I could be here at least an hour. Maybe they'll let me paint the walls. Oh well. May as well wait and see who comes through the door next.

"Hefty signs pleaded *'Please take a brochure.'* None were provided. Hand-lettered sheets taped to glass cages sternly admonished patrons to 'PAY AT THE TIME OF SERVICE.' A pink unicorn stood guard over a sign-in sheet fastened to a clip-board without a pen attached. Efficiency ruled.

"Three probable patients with thin faces and hips wider than fireplace mantles labored toward the sign-in window to fill out insurance forms for liposuction or some other invasions as indicated or prescribed. Young, old and older waited. Coughs and wilted tissues decorated a few who waited for the ever-smiling presence to open the door to the inner-sanctum and call the favored patient with welcomed words, 'The Doctor will see you now.'"

Irony may come across as sarcasm, but the writer may not notice the difference. Since people have various impressions of what they read based on their own experiences, editing can help assure a balanced reaction and the intention of irony or sarcasm can be better understood by the reader.

CHAPTER FIVE

Characters

"In the cold gray dawn the sisters lit their lamp and read their chapter with an earnestness never felt before, for now the shadow of a real trouble had come, showing them how rich in sunshine their lives had been."

- *Little Women,* Louisa Mae Alcott

Editors, writers, and readers expect a story that is full of interesting people, including those who are witty, stodgy, daring, attractive or just plain folks. Ultimately, editors and writers try to prepare a whole story about people who succeed against all odds and sometimes in spite of themselves. Writers try to explain who the people are, what they are doing, where they have been, where they go, how they react to what is going on around them or what dragged them to certain realizations. Editors attempt to assure that all of the questions that circle around the characters are clearly answered.

One overlooked editing flaw can make an entire chapter and a lot of hard work forgettable. Readers care about what happens. Valuable time spent with strangers who become part of readers' lives is justified or wasted. People written about become important. Physical dangers and impossible challenges take on varied meanings as each story and each set of characters engage or disappoint readers.

Writers, like readers, invest an enormous amount of time with ideas, words, and the process of moving characters from one climatic stress to another. Vivid descriptions and impatient presentations crowd through writer minds to either charm or disenchant readers. How an entire work is presented to various audiences can determine how well the work is received or how often readers reject it.

When readers are able to identify with or participate along with different characters, the writer clearly succeeds in the full creation and development of each individual. In literary or commercial fictions, biographical, historical, or autobiographical documents, people inside the tales being told must be made believable.

Every type of writing must engage readers in the lives of various individuals. When some attachment to the characters presented is developed among readers, the story can engage their imaginations. Readers expect to invest emotion and empathy for the people's lives they encounter through reading. Some readers involve themselves in the lives of fictional characters to the point that they feel they are actually journeying with the characters.

Unless the characters take on a life of their own, readers reject the people in the stories and refuse to become involved in their challenges or misfortunes. An editor's job is to determine whether or not the writing attracts readers. If there are dull or misleading spots, the editor must recommend changes accordingly. A writer's job is to listen to both editor and readers' responses and recognize when to make changes in the approach used in developing and presenting stories.

Both non-fiction and fiction stories ultimately revolve around different people, their thoughts, actions, and emotions. When the reader cannot distinguish one character from another, there is a problem. Stick figures and cardboard statues are shallow. Living reflections of active and important people are multi-dimensional and often unpredictable. Even characters created out of imaginations and formed by words must have substance. Edits can (or should) round out shallow characters and add unique personality quirks to any otherwise dull personage.

Personality and behavioral traits and can allow people to be brought to life by showing idiosyncrasies, speech patterns, fears, shortcomings, habits, or moral strengths. The fact that an invented character is only five feet tall may make him remembered more easily than if he were six feet tall in much the same way as a person who always wears purple may be more memorable than one who always is nondescript in the apparel chosen.

Play up unique qualities such as speech patterns, strange shoes, always whistling. Features or attitudes that can be made special adds to a remembrance factor and the substance a character brings to a story. Edits also make sure that each person is consistently the same. The six-foot tall blond with green eyes does not become the small brunette with dark eyes in later chapters simply because a few months have passed since the writer created the tall blond.

When developing a unique character, the writer can activate the reader's senses. For example: *"The bandy-legged droopy-eyed stranger spoke in a gravelly voice to the bartender. He gripped his whiskey with gnarled, rough hands. His clothes reeked of sweat and stale tobacco."* This description tells the reader that the stranger has had a rough existence, and is unusual in appearance. Who he is and why he is there may be mentioned sooner or later. If the stranger appears later, he is memorable. If he is never mentioned again, why he is included at all needs to be explained or the vivid description and the stranger's appearance need to be cut.

Descriptions can create a vivid, almost tangible person. When senses are triggered, often a reader can feel a bond with compelling characters. 'She always smelled of lilacs' is an overly stale phrase. 'She smelled like bubblegum' raises curiosity. 'We knew it was Jose because he was always whistling.' Some point of familiarity with each character improves association and recall.

Readers want to feel they personally know or have some sort of reaction to each character. When all the characters blend or mesh together, readers tends to become disinterested. Each character should be both complex and simple. Written characters are not on a stage performing, yet they should be presented so dramatically that even fast readers catch the full impact of each person.

Limitations and shortcoming make heroes human and evoke sympathy. A central character (whether good or bad) becomes the essence of the plot, but every Lone Ranger needs a Tonto sidekick. Building two strong characters is a challenge, but with clear separation of the identity of each, complementary acts and scenes add richness to most story lines.

Always mindful of the support given by a sidekick, the lead character must be more interesting, more doubtful, more heroic, more unpredictable, and draw more empathy than all of the other people in the story. Although others may rescue the main character, the hero must have a dilemma to overcome, a puzzle to solve, and trauma to survive. Even if the character is less than perfect or direly evil, the reader must be able to identify with the main character's longings, ambitions, failings and hopes of success. Sidekicks must be made visually recognizable, but should be identifiable through their habits and attitudes as well.

Each separate character needs an introduction with enough information to make them recognizable. Each person should support the plot without confusing the reader even when many sub-plots evolve from minor characters' deeds or mischief. Whenever any person is included, whether major or minor, an edit may uncover how that person adds to the story. If they are passing on the street, heavy description is unnecessary. If they support an action or an idea that re-occurs, more description is needed. Extra details added as the story progresses further enhance a character's individuality and promote more reader involvement.

When a character comes in and out of the plot, their appearance should be expected and the person should be remembered. A repeated check of when different people appear or how often a mention is made of certain characters may need to be made. Readers do not want to ask, *What happened to Joe?* Mentioned in an early chapter, but not included again for many pages, Joe's early and late appearances may need to be deleted. Or, he should appear more frequently in order to avoid confusion on the part of the reader.

Physical and mental descriptions:

A written portrait is more than physical descriptions or what kind of clothes a character wears. Readers want a name, some idea of age, perhaps even a place of birth. Some plots require the inclusion of residence (if any) by proximity, education level, religious inclination, parental involvement, spousal status, involvement of kids, any siblings, what kind of pets, or important friends.

Any or all of the important factual pieces of information may come into play immediately, or they may be introduced slowly as the plot demands. Past ancestry can become important if the story needs historical information. Hair color and shoe size may be important, but attitudes lend substance.

A profile of various characters shows what they are like outside and inside and allows characters to show different aspects of their personalities in differing situations. Attitudes reflected through moods and can explain actions. *Hemingway asked to be shown himself so clearly he would blush at his failings.*

Experienced writers answer the question, "What are these people like?" Experienced editors make sure the question is answered. A finished work shows the whole person in ways vital to the story. The flaws, struggles, ambitions, and passions show ethical or moral values. Hates or obsessions of important characters may be included. All of the secrets, weaknesses, strengths, wishes, pains, humor, financial condition, romantic inclinations, etcetera, of every character included in the story are available to the writer. Via editing, the characters become real and true to themselves.

Editors may help decide that too much trauma is included and there is no need for the reader to live through excessive gore or vivid pain. Miguel de Cervantes said Don Quiote was so obsessed with books, *'his brain dried up and he lost his wits.'*

The style of the writing reflects each character's attitude, education level, demeanor, and some of the physical attributes and even some of the life experiences of the persons through whom the writer enriches the story. The use of descriptions of what is happening to a character or what the character is doing or thinking adds flavor by including emotions, reactions to traumas, or other internal anxieties.

Caution is advised since what a character is feeling, thinking, or wishing can become distractions to the reader if internal meanderings of a character are overdone and become psychobabble. Including too much angst in any character's mental state may disrupt the story. An occasional swoop into the mind of a character can be richly insightful, but too many internal wanderings or shallow responses to serious situations can become obnoxious to many readers.

Conflicts:

Character conflicts must support the intent of the plot. A story is not limited to one character conflict, but some conflicts may be more prevalent than others. When considering character development, the writer determines what to focus on relative to conflicts. A work that follows an internal struggle such as a *'person against self'* conflict seldom has too many important characters.

A varying set of personalities may not be important if there is only one character reflected in the first person point of view. Other people can aggravate or prompt internal angst in a lead character who struggles against himself or herself, and others may be necessary to tell a full story even when only one person is the center of the story. Many autobiographical fictions focus on personality conflicts that may be psychological in nature and are most frequently written in first person narratives. Such conflicts do not exclude a variety of characters, but editing internal conflict works demands close attention to individuality of each person presented.

When all of the people who surround a lead character are well described and who have meaningful roles in the story, the end result can be both exciting and meaningful. Otherwise, careful editing needs to add substance to each person included, or the number of people involved needs to be lessened.

Every story and the various settings where most of the action takes place depend on the people involved. Once the theme and conflicts are chosen and the directions taken are decided, character development can proceed. Personalities can grow through involvements in different situations while the story unfolds. Actors on stage either stay 'in character' or get a scream from the director. Fictional people must consistently and continually stay 'in character' or the writer may hear a scream from the editor.

Thought patterns, ways of walking, of speaking, or moving relate to the age, experience, habits, or social connections of each character. Every person written into each scene must be well understood and clearly portrayed by both writer and reader. What a character thinks or feels may add flavor, but talking about what is thought is usually a stronger approach than straight descriptions. Short sentences in speech are more readable and more action driven than narrative.

All the attributes of each character need not be included at once. Bits of information scattered throughout can make a character more likeable or more threatening or more of a real person. It may take years for one person to know another person well. In literary and commercial fiction, it may take many scenes and many chapters to enlighten readers about the complicated background or abilities of a pertinent character. Many writers prefer introducing one additional person at a time. Editing is simpler when new people appear chronologically than when many important people are introduced in rapid succession. The old rule of three is a crowd holds true when too many personalities appear in one scene.

Writers who develop keen observation skills can add variety to draw on almost unlimited sources for descriptions of characters. One trait may represent one person and secondary characteristics support that impression as long as no two people are described the same way, unless twins or triplets are entwined into the story, but even then there must be some way for the reader to separate the identities. Watching, listening, and drawing mental pictures of different people and the way they sound or behave, provide both writers and editors important clues that can be used in character development.

Major characters:

The smaller the number of major characters included in any non-fiction or fiction writing, the greater the possibility is that each character has a greater impact on the reader. It's fairly common knowledge to farmers that crows can count up to seven before losing track of how many scarecrows are in a large field. Too many names, personalities, backgrounds and peculiar traits usually interfere with the story line and become confusing to the reader. Readers do not like to keep too many characters in mind as they wander through the lives of strangers who move in and out of a story. Few are better than many. Enough is enough. Too much is too much. When some characters are eliminated, the story can become stronger.

One, two, or three main characters usually can carry a fully developed plot. If the plot features multiple perspectives or more than one or two major characters, seven is a good maximum number. Draw the line against including others who may only mess up plots or become distractions that sabotage a story. Seven significant players are often too many for readers to digest. Edit out extras when possible, or combine actions attributed to two people into one person's behavior. Reduce three people into two, or keep combining until the actions are manageable and all of the people included are memorable and distinctive personalities.

Think about the number of people someone actually knows well. A person who has lived a long time may know a lot of people, but most people know only a few at a given time. The core amount (mainly close family members including those related to a spouse) generally stays the same. Friends and acquaintances, co-workers and neighbors come and go. Similarly, limits can be put on deciding which characters are significant to the story and to readers. A small number of major characters lend the possibility of having greater impact on the story and on audiences.

Minor Characters:

Characters guide and move the plot forward. It is vital to choose and develop characters and who are important figures in the story and necessary to the story. Although deemed minor to the story and action, no person is unimportant. Even the maid who only walks through a scene should be memorable.

Readers should feel they know each character personally. Being able to match each character to their physical description or expected attitudes avoids confusions. Readers shouldn't be asking themselves, "Who is this person and why is he doing that?" Many twists and turns and many scenes may have passed but each person mentioned should be recalled by the reader if or when he or she reappears.

Although insignificant compared with the luster of major characters, minor characters must be crucial to the plot while they support each other and the lead character. Minor characters breathe life into the story and add color to scenes. They open the door to how the rest of the invented world interacts with the major characters, and put the story and the other characters into perspective for readers. The more variety and uniqueness given to minor characters, the more vibrant the story will be, but useless and random additions of people who stumble in and around a story add nothing.

Writers generally do not state explicitly who has minor influence in a plot or sub-plot. Subtle awareness of a minor character may be all that is needed. All necessary characters have relevance if even barely mentioned. The famous actress Helen Hayes once said, "There is no such thing as a small part."

Some characters appear only once. They either add description or move the plot forward. If they appear at all they should be described and their presence should be explained clearly enough to be understood at least. There is little need to spend two pages describing the mailman who shows up once or twice, but readers should not be allowed to forget minor supporting characters only because their descriptions are so brief they are easily forgotten.

Robert B. Parker in <u>Chance</u> (Berkley Books, NY, 1997, p. 42) identified a minor character so completely that he was distinctly recognizable:

"Marty was a body builder, and a successful one, if you judged by the way his suit didn't fit. He was clean shaven with shoulder length blond hair and a dark tan. He had a small scar at the left corner of his mouth. And his right eye seemed to wander off center. There was a gold earring in his left earlobe, and a very big emerald ring on his right pinkie."

Almost a master at personality differentiation, Parker, in <u>Back Story</u>, (Berkley Books, NY, 2004, p. 186) gave a blatant profile of a person he obviously intended to remain in any future stories he concocted:

"Nobody looked quite like Susan. There were women as good-looking, though they were not legion, and there were probably women who were as smart, and I just hadn't met them. But there was no one whose face, carefully made up and framed by her thick black hair, glittered with the ineffable femaleness that hers did. She was informed with generosity and self-absorption, certainty and confusion. She was subtle and literal, fearless, hesitant, objective, bossy, pliant, quick-tempered, loving, hard-boiled, and passionate. And it all melded so perfectly that she was the most complete person I'd ever known."

Distinguishing between one personality and another may be a matter of the writer's style. Many characters are developed so well that some readers think they would be recognizable when (or if) they were ever met on the street.

Ethos:

When a character in a book behaves a certain way, has a phobia, or thinks uniquely, readers want to know they will be the same regardless of the situation in which they appear. The ethos of a person allows them to be known for whatever characteristic spirit they show or the beliefs they hold or those demonstrated. When certain attitudes or behaviors are mentioned, a necessary explanation may be included early in the story or left until later if an explanation heightens suspense or if an explanation carries action forward. At some point, however, each character must have both background and credibility. The ethos or distinctive 'spirit' of each individual should come through to the reader. If the person is always shy, make it known. If a person is always grumpy, let the basic nature of the grump be obviously consistent.

Credibility is added to the characters when motives for their acts are included. Did the youngster who had an irrational fear of dogs forget what kind of dog prompted his fears? Did he out-grow the phobia? Did his change support a new direction in his behavior? Can he become the real hero of the story after all?

Growth within a personality may take place, or a person may stay the same throughout regardless of the type of plot developed. The writer decides who the people are and how they behave, but the editor looks for inconsistencies or unexplained changes that add nothing to the story.

In a story that pinpoints psychological conflicts, specialized vocabularies are necessary. Behaviors or attitudes help tell readers who a person is and why they act the way they do, but the way in which a writer allows different behaviors to color the story and to promote sympathetic characters must be examined critically.

Villains behaving the way they are portrayed should follow reality. Some characters may be put into a situation that accidentally makes them the villain as long as the plot is supported. Writers describe criminals who exhibit weak resistance and become followers, or those not astute enough to know how to get out of untoward situations. Some criminals are described as sociopaths who prefer to go solo in all of their warped deeds. Other writers prefer sociopaths who commit dual or small group acts of violence or destruction.

If sect leaders are included, they must be believable in both demeanor and actions, otherwise the editing process should insist on expansions of descriptions or clarifications of acts. Sect leaders can be charismatic and entice innocents to follow unwittingly. Other sect leaders may be portrayed as committing ills toward the larger societies surrounding them. Nothing spells disaster as much as shallow presentations of specific roles.

Psychological terms used to describe criminal behavior are standard and many, but not all, are recognizable. Some of the less well known terms include: pederasty, the molestation of children; gerontophilia, attacks on older people; triolium, when one person watches while another sexually intrudes on someone else. If any specific term is used incorrectly or inappropriately, some readers will know the difference.

Medical and technical terms abound. Correctly edit some, delete others, or keep the particular field of expertise accurate with explanations as needed. When a writer uses a term specific to a field of study, readers expect to know what the word means or they want the word explained, or both.

If a long and unfamiliar word is used by one character, it is useful to allow another character to ask what is meant. This approach sets up the opportunity to explain what a word means. Some words used may make one of the characters sound stupid or uninformed, but may explain a character's behavior or background. Redundancy is helpful if it promotes clarity.

Edits should help make readers comfortable. Readers respond more favorably when the writer clearly conveys what is intended. When the words used, or the sequences of action are out of place, the story may need clarifications provided by sharp editing to avoid confusing readers.

Personality:

Personalities written about may be exuberant, or staid and unimpressive. Some may be sexy, powerful, evil or innocent, but all must be made complete and identifiable. The best writers allow readers to see people when they are presented through a kaleidoscope of variations. They write about distinctive people caught up in a multitude of events in differing places. Editors look for personal traits that make character more than paper cutouts. Readers want to know that the people who live in the pages are human and believably unique.

Each person in the story must have their own style, their own way of expressing themselves, and their own unique personality traits. When different characters are too much like each other in their acts and in their opinions, readers either get lost in the similarities or put down the story. When readers have to go back to an earlier section in order to find out who a person was, the first impression made was not strong enough. When too many similarities exist between various personalities, edit out any commonalities and introduce some exclusive traits or a particular physical identifier such as, *'She always cried when she wore green shoes.'*

Clichés:

Clichés are neither new nor fresh. Tired worn expressions add little to vital works. Clichés often interfere with establishing each personality as unique, but can be edited out when they are too well known, or changed to a fresh version of the same thought. 'A small leaf trembled' can be changed from the old thought of 'a dry leaf rustled' to promote suspense. 'She was pushed to the limit,' can be simply stated as, 'her spirit broke.'

Worn clichés get in the way of bright, crisp, action-filled stories. A 'well-oiled machine' sounds trite but can sound more dynamic than 'efficiently dangerous teamwork.'

Used as crutches when creativity wanes and time presses toward deadlines, writers resort to clichés. 'He was as old as Methuselah.' *'He was as brown as a berry.'* *'She was as quick as a flash.'* *'We will be together through thick and thin.'* While an aim of good writing is to enchant readers, clichés do more than enhance readers' boredom levels.

Clichés can hide deeper meanings snared into obscurity through the inadequacies of language. When emotions are more profound than a writer is willing to explore, generalities wrapped in clichés can envelope deeper meanings, but most clichés add little and are best avoided.

Stereotypes:

The beauty of fiction is that readers can suspend their own disbeliefs and widen their perspectives each time a new personality is encountered. But that idea only extends so far. Each person introduced in any fictional writing should be more than a stereotype drawn from a superficial two-dimensional portrait.

Writers who describe memorably individual characters understand the concept of typecasting, a form of stereotyping. Entire plots can be stereotypes. For example: the story revolves around a beautiful woman who hides behind horn-rimmed glasses and wears her hair pulled back in a bun. A long boxy suit over a white shirt with a tie hides her figure and the heavy shoes do nothing for her legs. A version adapted from <u>Sleeping Beauty</u> and <u>Pygmalion</u>, the determined but charming prince discovers her hidden beauty, takes off her glasses, lets down her hair and they both enjoy the transformation.

Writers and editors need to understand the concept and effect of stereotypes and the subsequent typecasting of characters. Regardless of the type of fiction being developed, stereotypes are useful but must be crafted with believability. Taken too far, stereotypes and typecasting weaken plots. Not every teenager is lazy. Not every policeman craves donuts. Not every banker is green with greed. Not every politician lies through their teeth (some hide their duality of purpose better than others), and not every grandpa loves to go fishing.

The more human the characters are, the more readers understand and identifies with them. Strange idiosyncrasies or behavior patterns have to tie in with both the character's background and the story as it unfolds. Readers have to care about the characters they meet on the printed page before being fully immersed in the story. Therefore, a mixture of diverse and engaging characters is essential to the vitality of any written work.

Characters become more interesting with more information added that expands their attitudes or experiences. Not all insights into a character's morals are included to make them more appealing. It is possible to offer details about a character in order to discredit them. Joseph Conrad's *Lord Jim* accentuates Jim's history and shortcomings. Even though Jim is narcissistic and cowardly, his heroic act at the end of the novel stems from his thirst for heroism and his need for self-redemption. Writers and editors learn form classical characters and their foibles.

Readers seldom want to read about a medley of people who have the same emotional reactions and identical personality traits. Variety and separation of identities must be believable even when the characters are 'over the top' stunningly unusual. Each person in the story who is significant enough to be highlighted must have their own hopes and dreams, sorrows and disappointments, intrigues and competitions, and their own way of expressing themselves.

Everyone has attended some gathering where there are a lot of people who are strangers. Some, however, are familiar and are remembered. Why are certain people memorable? It may be because of a distinctive name, a particular unusual habit, a vibrant personality, or a unique appearance. Even a special introduction of an otherwise unremarkable person could make an individual memorable. People are cemented into one's mind because of different traits, colorful outfits, or because they stimulated at least one of the human senses. They may have a shrill or croaky voice, or wore too much cologne. An otherwise traditionally dull social gathering can be made memorable if only one person stands out from the crowd or when a small exciting event takes place.

Character names:

Why particular names are chosen depends on the need to introduce or to convey a message about the character. The names by which they are known can add substance, betray their background, and reflect on the total person. Names have the ability to grab the reader's attention immediately, or they can be so complex that the reader easily forgets who the people are and why they were stuck into the plot. When carefully chosen, names add a mixture of cultural flair and heritage along with a bit of personality. When the writer ignores reasons for certain people to be where they are, the editor can put people where they belong or justify the displacement of what their names tell the readers. It makes little sense for Punjab, a native of rural India, to be named Eddie unless relocation and a name change relate to the story. Some writers prefer to check the history of regions from which names originate. A person in Wyoming named Aragon could be appropriate if time travel were featured, or if medieval names were part of the story. Otherwise, Seth or Chad would be better choices in Wyoming.

A fantasy or science fiction work usually demands outlandish or unusual names. It may be beneficial to give eccentric personalities a particularly peculiar name to add to the character's persona, but it may not make sense for people who live on a farm to be named Aragon or Whisperdona without a reason given as to why such names were chosen. Whatever name is chosen, consideration should be given to setting, background, and a point in time. When a name and a place are tied together, the writing appears more legitimate and a character is more easily remembered.

Names are meant to convey a message about the person. Some names add color and aid in identity. William Congreve, in <u>The Way of the World</u> uses associative names such as the wishful thinking woman "Lady Wishfort" and the devious, lying "Fainall." Descriptions of a person or what attitudes they have are easy to convey. Common terms such as 'squirt' may refer to a young or to slightly built person. A 'bulldog' of a man can mean that he looks stout and fierce. The options are many.

Short names are easier to write, to spell, and to remember. Not all individuals in the story should be 'Joe,' but neither should they all have long complicated names that are unpronounceable in the minds of readers who want to be able to recall and/or pronounce the comrades inside the books they prefer to read. During the process of editing, each name should be reviewed and checked for consistent spelling, for appropriate locale use, and for ease in recall.

Research:
Useful in editing, research helps check information not widely known. For example, it is beneficial to know

that some facts become obsolete and are replaced, while some facts seldom change.

In a 1969 article by Marvin E. Wolfgang, published in "Psychology Today," (pgs. 55-56 and 72-75) certain facts are valuable if a detective, suspense, or mystery is planned. On p. 74, Wolfgang stated, "Lower-class parents, especially fathers, strike their children or threaten to, more often than do middle-class parents." Wolfgang also mentioned that "Middle-class parents, in contrast, rely chiefly on psychological punishment."

If a writer needs to include data-based reality, Wolfgang's research showed that "the kitchen is where men are in more danger than women. Women kill their victims (who are almost always men) in the kitchen more often than in any other place, and much more often than men." Spousal slayings were, and still are, violent as well as numerous. "The bedroom has the dubious distinction of being the most dangerous room in the house. The bedroom is more dangerous for female victims than for males."

In the same study, Wolfgang wrote, "Most homicides are between males. Sixty-one per cent (61%) were male/male and only three per cent (3%) female/female cases." (p. 72.) Demographically, these profiles of behaviors have changed little in the past four decades, but a good edit does not rely on memories, old data, or current findings. Check it out.

Motives:

Psychological terms to classify or label behaviors have become part of ordinary vocabularies, thus motives or blatant reasons for different behaviors should be clearly understood by writer and by readers when any complex story unfold that describes acts based on aberrant behaviors.

David G. Myers states that "Research reveals many different biological, psychological, and social-cultural influences on aggressive behavior." (Psychology, Hope College, Holland Michigan, 2013, p.585). Influences can explain or lead to motives. Motives for behavior are important and should have explanations. For example: Carl, a killer, always leaves his victims near a creek, but never in the water. Why? Is Carl drawn to water but afraid of it? What does a creek have to do with Carl's behavior? Is there some significance to the creek or is it just a convenience to Carl?

Motives can be highlighted during the edit process, or at least suggested by minor inclusions. As the editing process unfolds, so does the reader's interest or lack thereof. Staying alert to ways that motives are hidden or made too blatantly obvious provide clues to improving a character's behaviors and can show ways to tighten or expand a plot.

Writers lose credibility when no explanations are given or when readers can't quite believe someone who has always behaved or talked one way suddenly changes. Either explain the change or delete the confusing behaviors.

Including details and explaining motives of every significant person throughout the story allows the writer to portray complete individuals who are more than shadows who come in and out of the plot. The emphasis here is on the word 'significant' and includes motives exhibited by each important person. While motives might be subtle or presented only through hints about what propels a person through a story, motives also reflect background and ethics or provide insights into a character's slant on morality.

Backgrounds:

Humans are complex beings who reflect their upbringing, their life situations, their knowledge, and their internal fears and uncertainties. Past events and current influences lend colorful meanings to their attitudes and behaviors. Education levels and skills blend with insecurities and doubts. A person in a profession that is dangerous will not act the same way as a person who has a steady, cozy, non-threatening existence. Personality steadiness or erratic quirks show up in awkward or dangerous situations and each reflects a difference in the character portrayed. How a character behaves and why they behave that way adds flavor or dull predictability to different situations.

Habits well defined and well scattered throughout different situations give depth of understanding as to who various characters are. Some writers build a complete biography or do a full-fledged resume for their main characters in order to keep consistency of presentation for heroes and/or villains. Both physical and attitude descriptions make complete persons who are distinctly individual. Some editors take notes on how each person looks and acts as a way to help identify inconsistencies throughout a long or complex plot.

The many reasons people do things may be unknown or mysterious, but become obvious only when pointed out. Quality writing, however, includes reasons or habits that underscore a character's actions. Motives that are left out but necessary to reader understanding must be urgently noticed and strongly suggested by editing. Include causative reactions in character developments.

The villain in a plot or sub-plot may be dysfunctional psychologically, but not be insane. Knowledgeable writers make distinctions between dysfunctional behaviors and insanity and show the differences. Edits should prove beneficial to clarify any confusion that interferes with reader understanding. Whether or not there is a legal connotation or if only a few details are missing and the scene is barely sketched without being complete requires a keen editing.

A villain may show compassion, warmth, and empathy but the absence of trust or some other sociopath tendencies must be evident in descriptions of the villain's motives, attitudes, or acts. To make a villain real through words shows profound knowledge of the types of people who maim or kill, who use rituals of torture, or those who display different personality quirks.

The individual who wants to blow up the pentagon may be on a power grab but otherwise be charming and well connected to celebrities and politicians. Readers want to know there is some justification for a character to behave the way they do. Both writer and editor must be aware of consistency and motive in each character's behavior and attitudes.

Frequent words used to describe molesters or killers include: insecurity issues, destructive, low self-esteem, lives alone or with parents past normal ages of separation, has limited social interactive skills, known to have killed or tortured animals at an early age, is secretive but may be intelligent, physically attractive, and seductive. Writers who limit their own vocabularies to describe various personality types and the behaviors they exhibit tend to limit the stories and the plots conceived.

Profiles of criminals are readily available to writers and editors, but profiles of victims are less common. When matching aggressors with a victim or victims, they should both be in plausible situations. Stay with motives and specific targets that match the character's customary attitude or behavior. Neither thoroughly presented villains nor victims should be allowed to go outside their particular characters just to make a story interesting.

Sean Mactire, in <u>Digest Books</u>, Ohio, 1995, wrote that basically there are three types of criminals. One is the average person, normal and balanced, rich or poor, the psychological make-up is not skewed to the point that it can be labeled as aberrant.

A second type of criminal Mactire describes includes those with personality disorders and behaviors that are personality based. Trauma is imposed on others because of some narcissistic and/or sadistic tendencies of the villain. The self-focused approach of narcissistic criminals bestows great havoc on individuals and on entire communities. There has to be a reason or multiple reasons for a character to act a particular way. When a character is supposed to be unstable, potential of the harm that person might do should be included. Otherwise, motives may be left out, overlooked by writers, and missed entirely by editors.

A second type of criminal or evil person may suffer from a biological or chemical induced malady. Substance abuse, chemical imbalances, physical illnesses, organic mental disorders, birth defects, and tumors of the brain are a few of the many recognizable affective factors which may lead to criminal behaviors. Writers who do not know the distinctions between the three larger groups described by Mactire can rely on self-editing research or go to an outside professional for guidance.

Heroes do not succeed until they overcome a formidable foe. Without including a strong villain, a story may lack a viable hero. Details can be included to demonstrate to readers that only a single cause is responsible for one character's actions, but others may have different reasons to act the way they do. Action scenes are fertile with excuses for characters to act in different ways.

Creating memorable characters is an exercise in totality. Whether the characters chosen are business associates, crime buddies, federal heavy-weights, bankers, local police, political figures, or a favorite niece, each can be complete in their attitudes and behaviors. If the people included are significant, they can be childish and selfish, filled with insecurities, live alone or with their families. Some people can be good neighbors yet be vile molesters or well-disguised killers. What becomes important is that conversation hints and dialogues in various situations can explain both how they act and why they do what they do.

Blatant interspersing of 'fly-on-the-wall' descriptions may be interesting or they may be inadequate and not carry the idea of what is attempted. Often, the best descriptions come from character's straight-forward quips of what they think about a person or place or event. Characters who throw pokes at each other add flavor to the story. Off-hand comments or sideline teases can add mood or expand the depth of a situation.

One remarkable trait can make a character memorable. When editing characters, look for something distinctive in a person's speech, clothes, hair styles, walks, or something as simple as a key chain. It may be only their teeth that help them stand out. Off-beat clothing or weird hair styles do not lend a dramatic effect just because they are included but more tension can result if an action includes descriptions. For example, *"He slung her over his scrawny shoulders and gripped her pink Mohawk-cut hair."*

The editing process should smooth out crowded scenes and make the people in each stage of the writing come alive. Conversations and confrontations usually intersperse dialogue between long descriptions of places, weather, or other necessary descriptions of place and time. Editing, or looking at the relationships of people to place puts the writer in more of an objective mode and allows a more critical examination of what is happening to the story as opposed to what is happening within the story. Editing helps surmount all difficulties.

CHAPTER SIX

Action

"You can't go back; go forwards. Don't dream; act!"

- *Proteus*, Morris West.

As a leading character begins a journey and overcomes dangers against all odds of succeeding, powerful stories evolve and suspense adds to a reader's compelling need to keep reading. Action happens. Verbs crowd together. Reactions shove toward the middle of what is taking place. People move. Emotions fly around. Ideas hide. Frustrations climb. Thoughts turn angry. Hatred asserts itself. Blood runs. Results push scenes forward. What happens in various scenes to different people support the major story line and expands the plot to cause excitement and build expectations. Action is drama! It is supposed to happen NOW!

When writing about action that took place years ago, the result becomes a passive, historical event that may or may not have any impact on what is critical in the present or what will be critical in the future. Something causes whatever took place in the past to be important in the present. Relationships between past acts, regardless of how long ago they took place, can tie to current actions and benefit both plot and characters' behaviors. Provided, of course, that any connections between past and present are valid and understandable.

Cause and effect actions lend motives to results by the consequences of what happens to various characters in specific situations. Momentum determines how the story unfolds. Whether or not it is dull, realistic, exciting, teaching or preaching, or just as the writer intended lends balance to actions taken. Editing helps assure that momentum continues and occurs in relation to the overall story.

Action reflects various tensions and danger levels as people are shoved through one scene after another of unexpected surprises or disappointments. The results of what happens to different people when they interact with others or with their situations must be put into words that convey action. Emotions displayed by or between people add depth to the story and allow the characters to show human traits in tough situations. If all emotions are excluded from an action scene, examine each interaction closely to determine where temperaments flair. Add richly appropriate responses during revision or editing.

Extra descriptive details can slow reader involvement to a standstill. Stopping in the middle of what's happening to explain why driving on cliff roads subject to rock slides is dangerous interrupts action. Telling about real or perceived dangers breaks the suspense. Editing out explanations and inserting psychological or physical reactions during various difficulties add tension.

Conflict is an essential element of each plot and sub-plot as the story unfolds while action is a tool used to increase reader interest. Disagreements, fights, explosive tempers or other confrontations add flavor and show possible twists in situations faced by one or more people. When editing action scenes, evaluate how often each scene supports the plot and how well suspense supports whatever action follows. Both suspense and action build on conflicts between major or minor characters and various characters' struggles against whatever difficulties are included.

Writers may be too engrossed in the story to analyze and edit uncertainty into various incidents or they may be unable to turn the story into suspenseful drama. Backing away from a scene to look at how many action verbs are used is one way to avoid being too absorbed in the story to know what needs to be done to improve the action included. There are many other ways to gain objectivity such as checking to find out when too many long sentences slow down action or when introspection by the characters interfere. Action scenes may be both short and brief. Intentional brevity is a way to keep action scenes interesting and filled with suspense.

How conflicts are settled depends on the story's focus and how events lead to resolutions. *How* things happen may be shorter than *why* things happen. No one component many be burdened with excessive detail, but readers expect to understand how, what, where, and why something takes place.

An impartial edit can shorten, tighten, resolve different approaches, or suggest ways to smooth out parts that could be more satisfying to both writer and readers. Each type of writing demands persistent editing even though action levels vary greatly between the different writing genres.

Action-filled stories are not limited to any one genre and every kind of fiction includes some kind of conflict. When opposing forces collide, the result is dramatic action. Astute editing requires some knowledge about what type of writing is being analyzed. The specifics of various kinds of stories and criminal collusions depend largely on the story's plot.

Mysteries include murders. Spy stories include assassinations. Horror stories include dismemberment or the returning dead or both. War dramas feature guns and explosions. Supernatural plots have vague spirits and untoward events that promote fears and increase anxiety. Science fiction may have mechanical or electrical or other foes to greet and conquer. Regardless of the type of story, or differences in plots used, action runs throughout and increasingly dangerous situations help move heroes through exciting events. Lead characters must survive, and conquer every challenge.

Editing any kind of action-filled fiction involves checking how many times things go wrong, if there is enough reward for doing what is expected, and how traumatic the outcome is supposed to be. Conflicts and dangers can be realistic or super innovative but they should be balanced. If an action scene drags on too long, or if it is put away to fix later, it may never survive and languish as something to be ignored by readers.

Another edit probe into action scenes must focus on deciding how each character fits into each scene and why they do what they do. The people involved should be worthy of the reader's time to care whether some character gets killed in the process of trying to escape a dire event.

People, physical barriers, and events all cause delays and create confusions. Each scene must be examined. Passive verbs should be made into active verbs. Action scenes can be replaced or held until much later in the plot. Other scenes are improved when they take place in different locations with different characters or greater dangers. Some scenes should be deleted altogether.

Pace:

The number of action scenes within the story's plot and sub-plots determine the pace of the work. Pace also includes the rapidity with which shifts within the story take place. If the story and its progressions are too slow, the reader may lose interest. If the pace is too fast, readers may wonder what was left out, or what they missed, or even what they wanted to know that may have been overlooked either by the writer or by themselves. An edit may point out what is missing or what can be added to improve possible interest factors.

Urgency and a fast tempo build suspense and add excitement to most stories. But it is not enough to rely on a writer's sense of urgency. An action sentence is: "Al shouted at the policeman." Editing seeks out unintentional shifts from active to passive verbs that diminish urgency. To slow down the action, use "The policeman was shouted at by Al." Whether the need is to increase the pace, or to slow down the pace, both should be done intentionally and corrected to fit the need.

Including aggravations or destructive behaviors of various characters can move a story forward or dull the senses of the reader. When vague psychobabble or excessive descriptions are included too often or too rapidly, readers may care less about what is happening, and skip the section or just toss the writing aside. Rapid shifts and jumps from one place to another can confuse readers. Or, if the movement from one person or one emotional scene to another is too quick, a reader may wonder why something seems incomplete.

Intentional interruptions that spread out heavy conflict scenes filled with fast action may be teasers inserted to let readers wait to find out what happens next, or they may be steps toward new acts that build reader suspense. Otherwise, disruptions of action may need to be revised. When stops and starts are obvious, it is best to mark any points of immediate change needed, or give some indication that revisions may be made later.

Too many digressions, or even too many characters, are potential distractions. Also, readers may not be able to stay engrossed in the story or even follow when too many scenes skip from one place to another too quickly. Rapid shifts that are not obvious or confusing to a reader can still be improved during the editing process.

Both writer and editor should be alert to the need to carefully show why or how a shift takes place. When a character moves from one location to another, or when other characters arrive on the scene, the shift or transition from one perspective to another needs to be explained. One of the many tasks in editing is to discover and help repair any confusions caused by switching places or people too abruptly without explaining why.

Changes from place to place or from character to character can be simple or complex as long as the story line is kept and the pace of each shift is not jerky. Skillfully done transitions can move the pace forward by dialogue or some mention that action has moved to a different time, place, or that other people have entered the scene.

Simple shifts between different scenes usually are made by extra spaces between one scene and the next. Or, some printer's mark can be inserted. The most commonly used approach in commercial fiction writing is to end one chapter and begin another on the next page. During edit sweeps, which form is used depends on the writer, but the editor assures that the form is consistent throughout.

Involved explanations as to what is happening do not add much to most stories. It is often better if dialogue is used to explain whatever it is that needs clarifications. Preference to one approach or another depends on an individual writer's style, what story is being told, and what value is added to an action scene by changing places or people. The purpose of any action scene must be kept in mind during the editing. Thinking about what impressions are made on readers can be used as a guide when deciding that an even but exciting pace is developed or sustained.

One way to gauge the purpose of action is to remember the audience. Reporting facts is done for newspapers. Newspaper editors have different tasks than commercial nonfiction editors since newspapers have limits on inches and columns. Drama is the approach taken by play-writes. Written in a special dialogue style that is interspersed with movement, lighting, prop and camera instructions, dramatic writings require specific knowledge of how various sets of directions are included for those involved in stage, screen, or television productions.

Nonfiction works have accuracy or educational constraints to satisfy. Pounding certain attitudes at readers in order to get points across may lose readers rather quickly. An instructional approach teaches but is best done in how-to manuals or textbooks. In literary or commercial novels, readers tend to prefer gentler pushes toward understanding new information. An escape from every-day dilemmas may be what brought the reader to the work originally.

Novels, made possible by quality story telling, are the mainstay of fiction writers who describe believable settings, unravel challenges and include actions that clarify the intentions of each character. Writers and editors have to assure logical presentations of interesting facts interspersed with various personality types and historical information. Multiple characters in exciting scenes add flavor to keep up momentum, but balance is more important than stuffing various people into dangers that don't strengthen the overall story.

An edit to examine the pace is a matter of going back over almost all the material. When a substantial amount of the writing is completed, many writers take the time to look over the work and add or delete or change around what seems out of place. Individual preferences come into play whether a work is edited as it is written, edited when it is thought to be completed, or edited when it is set aside and allowed to gather dust after being written. Each approach has advantages.

Generational differences abound between writers and readers. Writers in the nineteenth and twentieth centuries usually included page after page of detail. Twenty-first century writers hasten to describe in short abbreviated sections only what is pertinent. The difference resembles the fifteen-second per view standard for television commercials of the early 1950's and the three-second per view standard for television commercials of the 2000 era.

Rapid action-filled scenes create a different effect than when action is slow to develop and too much explanation crowds out character moves. When there are too many rapid shifts from place to place or from person to person, the impression is that the writing is confusing with not enough information on whatever consequences occur. Quick and clear descriptions are better than a large number of brief, speedy encounters. Anticipating consequences is difficult but thinking forward may be necessary in order to describe the results of whatever action takes place. Most strong stories include consequences and do not leave readers questioning what results were supposed to take place.

Whether the action is fast-paced, or burdened with excessive detail, the writer builds strength from consistency of form. When a work starts with short scenes and abrupt or fast-paced action, the expectation is that the same swiftness will continue throughout. When a slower more methodical or heavily saturated with detail pace is the approach used, the same should continue throughout.

The editor examines the results of choices made and recommends any and all needed adjustments.

Suspense:

Small sections packed with action encourage the reader to keep reading. Excessive details can become clumsy and interfere. Short sentences and brief dialogues can pick up tensions and increase levels of suspense. One way to make sure readers feel the tensions or despairs that hold a character is to raise the level of what is at stake. During edits, assure that the results of 'what if' factors are included. Some circumstances have damaging consequences if things go wrong.

Statements that build suspense at the end of a section can set the pace for the beginning of the next section or the next chapter. Allow for something that can continue to encourage interest and serve as teasers to reveal just enough at any one time to keep the reader engaged. One kind of tease is the suspenseful question: *"Will the bomb under the chair explode while the two men talk about baseball?"* Questions work when used sparingly. Too many questions add little.

Good writing shows action without telling about what action took place. Alert editing makes a distinction between explaining what is going on and showing what takes place. Compare a plain description with action statements to decide which prompts suspense and which can be deleted.

Telling what happened:

She lost control and the car went over the cliff. Found three days later, she was barely alive.

Showing what happened:

She almost moved her bandaged head and whispered. "Brakes…brakes didn't.." Half asleep, she raised a bandaged hand and mumbled. Her hand dropped. Her eyes tried to open. "Nobody wants to kill me…nobody."

Thoughts of characters added to raise questions are effective suspense elements that create wonder about what may happen next. Raising suspense levels can keep readers interested in outcomes. One way to check levels or frequency of suspense is to count how many pages come between jarring moments. When an edit shows that too much time goes by with no action, changes may be needed.

Suspense differs from drama but similar results can be produced. Drama adds interest and gets attention. When facts and movement come alive, the effect is to turn ordinary thoughts or events into dramatic situations that keep the reader interested. Some unexpected shock adds lively intent to thoughts or acts that may be uninteresting when told in a straight forward manner.

An unexpected interruption of the ordinary sequence of the activities of the principal character can create suspense. Minor characters or sub-plots can heighten suspense if intertwined in scenes that logically follow each other. Switching from one scene to another or from one time frame to another, if not carefully done, may add suspense or may only confuse the reader.

Timing:

Timing is an integral part of action. Timing in support of the plot or sub-plots means much more than setting a clock in motion to fight against some deadline at some future point. Many stories base their entire action on meeting a critical deadline. In those cases, the theme is meeting the deadline. Other plots require a different pace that reflects either time dragging or time accelerating. All writing and all editing take differing approaches, but awareness of what kind of pace is important to the story keeps the integrity of the work constant.

In building or in evaluating action through timing, descriptions play an important role. If there is too much detail included, either of place or of people, the action may drag. Each story and the way in which it unfolds must carry its own weight. This includes when the challenges or disappointments of its characters are introduced along with when conflict resolutions take place.

The skill of the writer/editor is evident in the use of what kind of descriptive phrases are needed and what types of unique settings are essential when dramatic action is needed. If the timing is unrealistic, a reader may think the entire story is superficial. If the time it takes to complete one or another act is impossible, the story may be perceived as disjointed. When actions are not creditable, the risk taken is that the rest of the material is not worth reading.

Elements evaluated during editing include emotions such as uncertainty. There are times when a person needs to act immediately. Sometimes introspection is needed. No matter what emotion is described, the reaction and the resulting actions must be appropriate to the character, to the situation, and to the story as a whole.

It is not easy for a writer to stay objective when the demand is to improve a work which spins a tale too close to the writer's own mental view of the world, or to the writer's passions. Objectivity in the edit process can point out that the work is a page-turner, is too dull, is realistic, is too full of psychological melodramas, the total effort has too many flaws, or none at all. The entire work may be excellent, consistent, rendered perfectly, and ready to publish as it. It still needs an objective edit review.

Decisions made and action taken directly relate to the situation posed and the people who respond to whatever trauma they face. For example: Marines are noted for moving on and for not spending a lot of time babying themselves or mulling over the philosophy of disrespect. Marines usually act or get mad. Teenage girls may cry or talk to all their friends about what a terrible burden not having the right dress becomes. Mothers may stew and stew over impossible situations and do nothing. Private detectives may ponder and think out a plan silently before they do something. Edits consider if actions taken are appropriate to each person.

Character backgrounds plus situations encountered dictate what kind of emotional reactions are included and how long or varied each scene should be. Editing entangled reactions may be a struggle when there is fast paced action and each scene gets full of tensions and dangers. In order to heighten action, the writer should shorten timeframes and figure out how to increase tensions among the characters or even include dread about future events. When characters worry about unknowns, their fears and imagined plights often spill out to a reader, but too much worry and too much "playing the victim" gets tiresome in the best of action scenes.

Cuts made during editing either move the pace along or they cause gaps in the story. Other cuts increase the pace. A writer may decide that certain large amounts of information are too important to cut. The editor/writer may decide to break up the information and spread it among different scenes. Deleting critical information may change the pace of entire sections of a book. Decisions as to the worth of what stays in or what is deleted need to be based on how well some points can be integrated into specific scenes or how well dispersal of information can improve the total package.

One approach is to spread action across several scenes but avoid disruptions or confusions as to who is included or what information is shared. Another approach is to decide that the entire plot is better off without some of the information. Scenes get tightened and action moves forward when critical cuts are made. Doubts as to whether information is useless or valuable can deter cuts. Pieces of scenes that seem to be necessary can be saved and considered for a later point in the story when doubts arise. Editors often put question marks in the margins to question the appropriate use of a sentence or of a section.

Editing action scenes usually means substituting long rambling sentences with short sentences to pick up the pace of what's going on. Changing pace from one crisis to another is expected. When the assassin peers through the window, suspense increases and dread mounts. If immediately the scene shifts to a sleeping child or to a maid stirring a boiling pot, the pace is interrupted, but tense reactions can remain. The wave of alternation between high action and calm retreats let readers catch their breaths and allows writers to figure out what comes next.

Beginning writers frequently try to interject as many action scenes into a story as possible, but unimportant scenes can crowd out more important ones. Unimportant scenes remain only if they do not overshadow important ones. Editors help writers select meaningful situations and include important decisions by characters as a way to determine which actions stay in a story and which ones interfere with the flow of critical information. Urgency plus fear or desperate calls for help may give extra details into existing or future situations and may allow additional insights into the people involved. Even one-sided conversations (such as phone calls) may heighten action levels or add conflict and suspense. Any approach that contributes to understanding what is going on can add depth to either violent or peaceful situations.

CHAPTER SEVEN

Dialogue

*The great act of faith is when a man decides
he is not God.*

-Oliver Wendell Holmes, Jr.

Dialogue shows personality, adds motion, and gives breathing room to blocks of descriptive narrative. Each conversation serves a specific and vital purpose where rules of grammar seldom apply. Most talk is a condensed version of thinking aloud. Written talk is an abbreviated reflection of the person speaking. Much is implied to convey information but each statement must be natural and believable to each character's personality and background.

Spoken words separate yet unite diverse people who talk to themselves and others. Conversations show personal differences in experiences or attitudes. A person's style of speaking reflects desires, defines levels of expertise, or generally keeps moving the story along. Provided, of course, there is some meaning behind the conversations and some reason for including them.

Dialogue must always serve a purpose. It can be used to give a description of the place where people meet to discuss the next murder or where they plan to have a lovely spot of tea. Rather than imposing straight descriptions on readers, include some talk. It's more interesting when conversations show what a place looks like and how the setting affects moods or explains individual reactions.

A romantic man might be interested in how the sunset seen through the window strikes his female companion's hair and casts a coppery glow. A woman who is far from romantic might describe the same sunset as a warning to get out of the place before dark. A richer sense of emotions and reactions can be conveyed through dialogue than through straight descriptions.

People talk certain ways and use different levels of formality. Each person's way of speaking and each character's method of using words should be different enough that readers can tell who is speaking.

A cantankerous ol' visitor can plant clues or add suspense or even become another element of a sub-plot or invade the larger plot to cause future disasters while muttering to himself or talking to others.

External dialogue:

External dialogue involves people talking to other people. Most of the conversations give useful information that moves a plot along its predetermined path. Meaningless conversations used as fillers seldom add anything to the bigger story. Valid conversations can give insights to personalities, motives, plans, or even unexpected actions. Every conversation can have meaning, whether it just adds description, or gives a forward kick to the action to come. When it doesn't add anything, delete it. An alternative would be to substitute words that show motives, contributes to a character's attitudes, or includes something of significance that would otherwise be missed.

Internal dialogue:

Internal dialogue usually means a person is reflecting on some abstract or even meaningless thoughts that scramble and tumble inside that person's head. Regardless of whether the thoughts are clear or confused, the reader needs to comprehend and follow the trend of what is happening and have no doubt as to why the person is ruminating on whatever goes on inside that person's head. When a character is hesitant about what to do, some delay in action may be needed to give one or more characters time to gather poise or decide what to do next. Edits must be are alert to necessary slowing down by using dialogue as a way to pace interactions of people and the moods conveyed.

Both internal dialogue and silent dialogue may be indicated by quotation marks, or internal dialogue may be included as general narrative and prefaced by explaining that someone is thinking. Thoughts used to cause doubts or to raise suspense levels can increase the pace of action or they can decrease tensions and slow down a character's hyperactivity. A useful approach, thoughts inserted at critical junctures may be a benefit or interject awkwardness. Whatever the result, whether it is beneficial or needs to be changed, internal dialogue is not the same as silent dialogue although the effects may be similar.

Whispers not overheard or not widely heard, talking or muttering to oneself in a crowd, or thinking out loud in an empty room are all silent dialogue. Usually typed or printed the same as regular conversation, the difference must be obvious to the reader or effectiveness is lost.

When scenes shift or people go to different places, silent dialogue can explain why things are about to change or have already changed.

Dialects:

Dialogue traps abound due to regional, national, and international differences and because spoken language is alive and evolving. Dialects express regionalism and individuality. Colorful language and unique reflections on different subjects add interest to any story. But, dialects have to be readable and understandable. When one wants to accomplish both, it is critical to make sure all of the spelling of each dialect word is consistent. The spelling can be awkward, different, or just plain wrong. But it must be consistently wrong or it becomes a major difficulty to edit.

Anne Perry's <u>The Face of A Stranger</u>, (Ballentine Books, l990, p. 2) reflects a typical British speech pattern of the late 1800's of a hospital worker who was not expected to know much more than how to greet patients and tend their bodily needs.

"You're a right one, yer are. Yer dunno nuffin' from one day ter the next, do yer? It wouldn't surprise me none if yer didn't 'member yer own name! 'Ower yer then? Ow's yer arm? Wot's yer name, then?"

On page 54 of the same novel, Anne Perry included the language of a building superintendent who knew how to address an officer of the law and give excuses for himself at the same time.

"Ah, there you 'ave me, sir; I don't think as I would. Yer see, I din't see 'im close, like, when 'e was down 'here. An' on the stairs I only looked where I was goin',' it bein' dark. 'E 'ad one o' them' eavy coats on, as it was a rotten night an' rainin' somethin' wicked. A natural night for anyone to 'ave 'is coat turned up an' 'is 'at drawn down. I reckon 'e were dark, that's about all I could say."

Grammar used by Anne Perry's nurse is different than that used by the building superintendent but both are unique to the place, period, and class. Notice that the *d, g,* and *h* are missing. Additions of local color and regional vernaculars heighten interest in both setting and plot.

Dialects give characters their own personality and helps bring them to life. When used well, dialect can add a unique quality to reading because it is almost 'heard' by the reader. But dialect is most effective when used sparingly. It can add character definition and enhance reader interest, provided clarity is kept. When editing, be sure all dialects used do not confuse the reader and add interest rather than being a distraction.

Shakespeare used words like 'perforce' and 'whilon.' Current writers use 'necessarily' or 'once' instead of Shakespeare's words. The word 'Thou' or 'thee' is still used in special places, in certain religious writing, or even in a few special communities. Unless a particular circumstance calls for the use of the word 'thou,' the more common 'you' is preferred.

Language that reflects the age, stage of life, experience, and attitudes of different speakers gives authenticity to the people who scatter their lives across the pages being read. Teenagers show an exaggerated pronunciation of any regional dialect that may be used by their parents. People who have traveled widely, or who have lived in widely separated parts of a country tend to lose their local dialects. Broadcast personalities have less of a local accent than farmers even when both groups grow up in the same small town. Professors of higher education usually lose most of their local dialects because they spend so much time talking to a wide range of people.

Whoever is talking, in whatever scene, should be clearly identifiable. If age and level of experience are unimportant at a particular point, try to write words that show who the person is and why they say the kind of things they say. When writing dialogue, the sound of a local accent can be replicated through spelling. Authenticity can be verified when dialogue is read aloud. If it doesn't sound right, change it.

Writers who engage in casual eves dropping ordinarily write better dialogue. Practice in listening to the way others speak may improve the way writers write. The individuality of each person who talks to others is similar to what many writers find when they sit on a bench somewhere and listen to passing strangers talk. Each person speaks their own way and reflects their differing personalities and their experiences. Educational levels are discernable when people talk. Regional geographic distinctions or variations between urban and rural can be distinctive. Backgrounds and experiences come alive with vivid dialogue and behavioral traits well described.

Conversations are made up, but they mimic everyday use. If stilted, or too formal, there must be a reason why characters talk the way they do. Variety of language use is always best among the different characters as a way to make each person distinctive. When every character sounds like every other character, readers will notice. Writers and editors cannot ignore the lack of uniqueness among the people talking. Characters who come across as shadows of each other must be changed (unless, of course, they are twins).

Some people are very casual in their habits of speech and the style of life they pursue can be reflected in their style of speaking. A butler to the master of a British manor will be expected to have a formal style of speaking. A street-smart gang member from lower Brooklyn will be expected to have a colloquial style of speaking. The conversational style used can add a great deal of interest to any writing and an alert editing will capitalize on the differences available.

Natural conversations reflect the peculiar portraits of people who have lived unique lives under unique circumstances. The way people talk to themselves or to others also reflect their occupation or give insights into the lives of ordinary folk who have met with unique circumstances. Speech can be a reflection of the way people live or it can tell about their attitudes, their tendency to be secretive, bold or submissive, or just plain evil. The way people talk and the phrases they use tell a lot about various personalities, which locations they are from, or if they lived in other periods of time.

Clive Cussler presented a specific portrait of a stranded seaman who probably talked the way he wrote, or so his message seemed.

"Me mind is as set as a stout ship before a narth winde. I shalle not retarn to mye homelande. I feare Captaan Drake was maddened for ne not bringen the achant tresures and the jade boxe with the notted strings to Enland soos it cud to preezentid to guude Queen Bess. I left it with the wracked ship. I shalle be baryed heer among the peapol who have becume my family. Writen bye the hande of Thomas

Cuttill, sailing mastere of the Golden Hinds this unknown day in the yeare 1594." - Clive Cussler, <u>Inca Gold,</u> N. Y., l994, p. 206.

The old seaman conveyed his situation and his lack of education as he accepted his last days. By adding the note, what happened to the old man was clarified and the story moved forward.

Occupational dialogue:

Occupational speech can reflect personalities and set apart life style differences. A football player may say: "I should of..." A Professor may say: "I should have..." A Teenager may blurt out: "I ought've..." A Ranch hand may say: "I shoulda..."

Baseballese is a language unto itself. Columnist Red Smith called baseball talk "...a live language only superficially resembling Sanskrit." Sports words are a foreign language to those who know nothing about a particular sport or who do not watch the never ending parade of televised sports. But jargon, the special language used by different trades or activities, is not limited to sports commentators. A writer can 'screw around' or 'screw up' or even create all kinds of 'snafus' just by not paying attention to the language used, or ignoring the audiences intended. An editor wants whatever is said to be readily understood even when specialized words are used.

Jargon or slang highlights certain groups, and used effectively distinguishes one character or one group and makes them more memorable. If jargon and slang are used inappropriately or repeatedly, or when they are assigned to people who do not usually engage in off-beat words, they can confuse a reader and must be checked for usefulness.

One way to check funky dialogue is to match its style to the person speaking. When jargon or slang sounds artificial, it should intended to sound that way, as in irony or poking fun or blatant insults.

Many people move around when they talk. Descriptions of place or attitude or weather can be added as a character moves. Short interspersed asides can benefit both the story and the readers who expect to have their own emotional responses to characters. Comments may be included about something in the past or in the way a person is dressed to add depth and identification to speakers.

Variety is always a stronger approach than using tired old-style tags. Conversation tags take up more room than most writers want, and take up more time than most readers expect. Tags are useful and necessary but they do not have to be overdone. A tough edit can delete 'he said' and 'she said' used in every statement and substitute descriptions of what they are thinking or what they see while they talk.

Every line of dialogue must have some way for readers to easily distinguish between talker and listener. Readers do not want to go back to find out who 'he' or 'she' is talking, nor do they want to get confused by which person is talking at any one time. Writers can clearly identify who is speaking, or give some other indication of who is who when extra information is added such as *'John sneered as he poked at the cold pizza.'* Hand motions, smiles, body movements, distraction, thoughts, attitudes, giggles, or other nonsense can add identity to whomever said what.

Dialogue lets the reader know who is present and what is taking place. Too much 'he said' or 'she said' wastes time and gets in the way of the movements needed to convey action. It can be just as clear when little descriptions are included such as 'she moved uneasily' or 'he stomped his foot when he answered.' 'She answered, but her nervousness was obvious.' During editing, alternative paragraphs are used to distinguish between speakers.

There are many, many ways to simplify and to clarify meanings that are supposed to come across through dialogue. One good way is to trim out the fat of each conversation. Words that are added to give emphasis to some thought are more acceptable in spoken language than in written language.

In narrative writing, repetitions are considered fat. In writing dialogue, the character doing the talking takes the stage. Speeches that have to be part of the story use a special type of dialogue depending on who is making the speech to how big an audience. When speeches are included, most should be brief and sprinkled with short funny words or jokes. Most speeches use a formal tone. If a politician speaks as part of the plot, some snide comments may be made by a character standing nearby. There is little need to repeat what has already been clearly written, however, unless a preacher character gets carried away and continues to bomb-blast his audience with repetitions.

Variety added during the rewriting or editing provides choices. Writer/editors can slip in absurd exaggerations to expand a character's personality, explain an event, or shift attention from one person to another. Unexpected words often catch reader attention and are a good tool used during the editing process.

Regardless of the story, the characters, or the settings, all dialogue must be included for a reason. Conversations can show insights into various characters, can lead to suspenseful scenes, or even let readers anticipate what is going to happen. In real life, people seldom talk much and others ramble on without saying much worth hearing. Characters must be believable in whatever is said and both tone and content must be appropriate to the time and place in the story. Regardless of style or accent, conversations must reflect the atmosphere of the plot and be necessary.

Attention-getters, emphasis, and exaggeration all go together. Strong words and flat statements are attention-getters. A tough or strong character can get away with strong words but it gets a reader's attention when a sweet little ol' lady comes out with a strong flat statement. A diplomat can hover between appeasement and toughness in speech while bums are not expected to be proper. Soft words can be stuck between strong reactions and tough verbal responses.

Exaggerations:

In 1960, the Famous Writers School in Westport, Connecticut, published a series of courses under the guidance of Director, Gorgon Carroll. The courses still have valuable content five decades later. In volume I, Section II, lesson eight, pages 153, 154, and 155, Emphasis and exaggeration are soundly illustrated as follows:

"...another technique related to emphasis is exaggeration, a favorite style device with many writers. Charles Dickens used it with good effect, as in the passage making fun of a poor financial risk (from '*Little Dorrit'): A person who can't pay gets another who can't pay to guarantee that he can pay.*"

Mark Twain constantly used exaggeration as a technique to drive home points dramatically, as in <u>Life on the Mississippi</u>: *"Sired by a hurricane, dam'd by an earthquake. . . I'll learn him or kill him." "The educated*

Southerner has no use for an r, except at the beginning of a word." Or in <u>The Adventures of Tom Sawyer</u>: *"There were some that believed he would be President yet, if he escaped hanging."*

George Bernard Shaw used exaggeration effectively. In fact, his readers came to expect it of him. In the following, from <u>You Never Can Tell</u>, Shaw quipped: *"We don't bother much about dress and manners in England, because as a nation we don't dress well and we've no manners."*

Will Rogers was near the top of the list of those who used exaggeration to emphasize a point. The following are from various newspaper columns Rogers wrote while traveling all over the world.

"It was an impromptu address he'd been working on for only six months."

"Legislatures are kinda like animals in a zoo. You can't do anything about 'em. All you can do is just stand and watch 'em."

"People couldn't have been as nice to me if I had died."

"A bunch of American tourists were hissed and stoned yesterday in France, but not until they had finished buying."

Red Smith was an addict of the exaggerated style. His columns included: *"Stengelese (a baseball manager's talk) is a live language only superficially resembling Sanskrit."*

"I never shoot a deer, unless he pulls a knife on me."

Exaggerations emphasize ideas and put them across in the relative importance as intended. Fundamentally, exaggerations say something so absurd that readers can't miss the point. Ring Lardner made a memorable comment when he wrote of a lovesick ballplayer: *"He gave her a look you could of poured on a waffle."*

Repetitive dialogue:

It is a heavy task to expect the edit process to make sure that every word of dialogue makes the point that the writer intended. One of the rougher tasks is to write as if different people are thinking, behaving, explaining something, or even allowing insights into the hidden parts of a mind. Aware of differences and subtle suggestions made between characters keeps the editing process fresh and lets the writer and/or editor stay tuned to the nuances of various words.

Repetitive dialogue, used by Hemingway in his short story, *The Killers,* established a new approach to the use of dialogue that has been widely used since the beginning of the twentieth century. The story is about two gangsters (Al and his friend Max) who go into a café to find a guy they want to kill. They sit at the counter and heckle George the counterman and customer Nick Adams. Abstracted from 'Good structure in writing, p. 141, ibid., the following is a sample of Hemingway's style:

"Got anything to drink?" Al asked.

"Silver beer, ginger-ale," George said.

"I mean you got anything to *drink?"*

"Just those I said."

"This is a hot town," said the other. "What do they call it?"

"Summit."

"Ever hear of it?" Al asked his friend.

"No," said the friend.

"What do they do here nights?" Al asked.

"They eat the dinner," his friend said. "They all come here and eat the big dinner."

"That's right," George said.

"So you think that's right?" Al asked George.

"Sure."

"You're a pretty bright boy, aren't you?"

"Sure," said George.

"Well, you're not," said the other little man. "Is he, Al?"

"He's dumb," said Al. He turned to Nick. "What's your name?"

"Adams"

"Another bright boy," Al said. "Ain't he a bright boy, Max?"

Ernest Hemingway continued to develop the horror that crossed a small town through repetitive dialogue uninterrupted by descriptive detail. There are fallacies, however. Even in the brief lines included here there is confusion. "The other" mentioned leaves doubt as who the 'other' is at this point. "His friend" is used three times and is as confusing as the "other little man."

As important as repetitive dialogue is as a tool, writers and editors should keep a skeptical eye on the pace, the completeness, and any careful distinctions between characters needed to keep clear just what is happening.

Word origins:

The origin of a term or a phrase may not be known by either a writer or the editor. At times, however, knowing where a word or an expression comes from is useful. Sources or originations may help even those who are knowledgeable enough to keep from pitching red sox into a washing machine along with white T-shirts. For example, "That won't wash" probably dates from around 1840 and was used by Charlotte Bronte (1849) when she was quoted in the Oxford English Dictionary 'That willn't wash, miss.'

The phrase originally referred to undependable dyes used in fabrics but the term came to mean 'It won't work' or 'You're not telling the truth," or 'I don't believe you.' Ever alert to shifts in meaning, an edit can find statements that are misleading. Finding changes that need to be made requires diligence and willingness to find out when a phrase or a simple word is incorrectly used. Some prefer to ignore the hard tasks of seeking word origins and erroneously pretend no one will notice if mistakes are made.

CHAPTER EIGHT

Structure

"When you get to the end of your rope, tie a knot, and hang on."

-President Franklin D. Roosevelt

Straightforward stories are easy to read. A simple and cohesive story is seldom easy to write. The plot may move along one central idea and all of the words, sentences, paragraphs and sections may hold together. Without any bumps or twists in the mixing together of the diverse elements there may be a story that holds interest only to a few. When each element is well crafted and appropriate to the setting chosen, it becomes a mystery as to how it happened, but most of the time the result is excellent and both writer and editors are surprised and pleased.

Editing questions usually do not interfere with recreational reading, but glitches and stumbling blocks can be found when a story is examined critically. Some questions that guide the editing process include:

1. Did the writer keep the reader involved in the story and describe each move clearly enough that the reader did not get lost along the way?
2. Are the transitions clearly defined in order to sustain interest on the part of the reader?
3. Did the writer prevent boredom from setting in and losing the reader in the process?
4. Does the writer keep a consistent and clear approach to who is doing the thinking, or doing the acting, or going from place to place.
5. Does switching from one tense, one voice, or one character to another create doubt in the reader?
6. Is there a purpose to changes made?
7. Do dialects or foreign phrases enhance or detract from the story's purpose?
8. Are there too many worn out phrases or tired descriptions used?

Answers decided upon quickly give the best response to actual reactions. When there are too many *yes* answers to the above questions, a sad conclusion is that the story is a mess and can be discarded as it is presented. The approach taken in critical editing is to examine how the story is presented and to anticipate how well it will be received.

Editing scrutiny includes tireless sweeps to correct major and minor errors, repeated revisions and elimination of distractions. Logic is reinforced to make sure action scenes are realistic and each word chosen remains coherent. Each sentence is examined to close any gaps between moves from one idea (or place) to the next. Some paragraphs may be too short to make sense.

Other paragraphs may be too long and become tiresome to the reader.

Editing structure is the process of looking for any fallacies in approach and in content that may disrupt the flow of the story. In writing fiction, the story is the most important consideration. The purpose of editing structure is to enhance the story and improve the total work. Analysis and examinations are two important approaches to use while the whole structure undergoes scrutiny.

One way to analyze the structure of a plot is to make a diagram that connects the relationships of the major events included. The diagram may be a chart or a simple list of the four or five major points of the story. Overly complicated diagrams or lists may indicate that the plot is too complicated. The reverse can be helpful. Recognizing that a diagram is too simple may mean that the plot needs more twists or turns. When only a few narrow escapes are included, add additional or more dangerous events. Added shifts or surprises can increase reader interest and provide an excuse to include more details.

Core editing:

Core editing focuses on the mechanics of structure. The writings can include adventure or mystery or romance mixed and blended to support different people in various situations. A core edit process helps make sure that everything included leads to a finale that ties all of the components together into a climax.

After checking and re-checking all of the various details numerous times, it is still necessary to examine how the whole of the work is put together. An overview may be easy to do at this point, or it may become impossible due to the many revisions already accomplished. Initial writings include presentation of an idea. Rewriting based on structural weaknesses involves shifts in emphasis, order of sequences, expansions of scenes or refinements of character involvements. Critiques of any improvements or changes made can lead to further stern revisions and many polishes, hence the need for re-checking.

An examination of structure includes looking at *how* various pieces fit together. *What* is included depends on the story and ways in people and their actions flow. The underlying structure holds together the scenes and the results of all the traumas to determine if they fit together like interlocking pieces of a jigsaw puzzle. Unity and believability are apparent when the structure is logical. Various details that are included early in a story and subsequently forgotten or intentionally omitted can distract or confuse. Creditability can intertwine with plots and sub-plots or can be lost in ignored structures.

A writer/editor looks at the overall integration of events and people as the story progresses. Exaggerations of actions or dialogues and distortions of time and place have subtle but grave effects on the polished condition of the writing and on reader responses. A stilted academic approach can stifle both non-fiction and fiction. Too flippant or too casual an approach can cause a weak reputation to be assigned to a writer and condemn a work before it has a chance with professional editors or publishers.

A writer may be able to stay objective enough to make solid examinations. An editor's task is to carefully examine and to make valid suggestions for any improvements or clarifications. When a writer becomes the editor of one's own work, taking a bit of time off from it can be useful.

A work that is looked at after a period of time often can be seen more clearly than when it is freshly written.

Structure Elements:

Editing steps done in examinations of structure include separating different focus points into five different elements. For effectiveness in edits, each has its own examination. There may be other elements to consider, but for purposes of close examinations, the following are beneficial:

1. Places, 2. Persons, 3. Plot, 4. Purpose, and **5. Theme.** These five elements may be examined at the same time, or they can be separated and examined one at a time. A review all of the components together is more difficult and usually causes the examiner to get lost in the details. The following are both definitions and points to follow in critically editing each component.

1. **Places** or settings include every place where various characters do whatever it is they do. Place descriptions must be sharp and necessary.

2. **People** or characters throughout the story constitute the core around which the plot revolves. People must be clearly individual in their thoughts, appearance, and actions.

3. **Plot** includes interactions of people and places which constitute the problems to be solved throughout. Plot, sub-plots, or back-stories must be believable.

4. **Purpose** or the reason why a particular story is written. The purpose of telling a story must be greater than writing for the sake of writing.

5. **Theme** or the message of the story. The theme of what is written may only be implied through the story itself without preaching about what should be subtly understood.

Each section of substance and form can be reviewed for structural flaws. Many of the suggestions will apply to non-fiction writing and polishing efforts of short stories or other writings as well. While it is critical for all writers to correct their work, the emphasis here is to prompt meaningful examinations of each section of a piece of writing before it reaches whatever public it is designed to enlighten.

The editing function is one of analyzing. When distinguishing between who is talking and who is listening, find out what is repeated or what is missing that needs to be added. Examine substance by questioning different elements included but that may be out of sequence. Keep looking at whatever is written from the reader's perspective. If it satisfies, keep it. If it is off the mark, change whatever is not right. Ways to integrate each separate part become conspicuous to the editor who has a practiced level of observation.

Reading through a section can increase focus on particular areas. During a read-through, circle words that could be stronger or clearer. Replace the weaker words. Another read-through can focus on an examination of the plot. Do the efforts involved by various characters (especially the lead) get more and more difficult? Is failure certain? If not, why not?

The work of skilled designers, those who create masterpieces of merit, whether they leave magnificent sculptures, rare fabrics, ancient manuscripts, or books to read and re-read, appeal to both novices and experts. Experienced musicians can hear false notes. Musical conductors know how to blend soft sections among faster or louder sections to please their own sense of balance with the reactions of an audience. Conductors require practice even from talented and experienced professionals. Successful classical and modern writers who satisfy their readers seldom disappoint. All artisans try to reach a high level of perfection. Some succeed. Others do not. Editing along with many reviews usually make the difference.

Writers whose compositions have flawed sections and awkward integrations get criticisms and their works may hold little or no appeal to either novice or expert readers. Rewrites and an almost compulsive need to edit help move both novices and advanced writers to a higher level of competence. Editing may be called 'compulsive' because it seems never to be completed. There seems always to be some word, or phrase, or punctuation mark that stays out of place even after multiple revisions.

Reviews of settings and scenes help avoid mistakes caused when out of place or out of time sequences are included or some description of what a character is wearing is mistakenly changed. In movie-making, the person who makes sure that the same shirt is worn by the same person at the same time of day during the next film session is called a "Continuity Editor." Writers and editors must be aware of continuity throughout printed materials and assure that constancy is maintained.

Inconsistencies cause the reader to question the credibility of the writer when blatant contradictions appear regardless of the type of style of writing. If a particular character has a phobia that involves lake water, it is puzzling when that person takes a dive into a lake for a recreational swim. If a transformation takes place (perhaps the character overcomes the fear) readers must be told why something changed that allowed the lake swim to happen. Without a clear explanation of the change and why it happened, the scene can come across as disjointed. With no obvious continuity, the total work is weaker. A writer/editor benefits from keeping a good eye out for inconsistencies and flaws when action moves from one scene to another.

Rapid shifts from one location to another must be understood by readers and explained by writers. If there are high mountains in the distance yet to be climbed, keep the momentum going or at least let readers know why scenes shifted or why the mountains suddenly turned into dusty plains. Ruthlessly cut unimportant details or add more information that includes explanations or helps clarify.

Obstacles:

Many of the obstacles encountered in a final edit relate to the structure of the work. Others include the attitudes of the writer which can become a major drawback to the editing process. Attributes that get in the way of being objective may include the writer's personal habit of resisting any suggestions for improvements in what is written. The popular phrase, "Get over it!" may describe how edits become salve to a writer's ego when pet phases get cut. Cuts of mundane statements can benefit the overall work just as the addition of extra information can flush out some unfinished section. A good edit may eliminate some of the personal foibles of a writer, but others may need to be overcome.

When possible, writers need to avoid being full of stern stubbornness or totally rejecting anyone who tries to make suggestions or changes. Flexibility in attitude on the part of the writer is a major asset in editing. The target in any review of every work, regardless of how long or how complicated, is the audience and improving the chances of eliciting positive responses from readers.

How well any written work is put together is evaluated by many critical judges. To move from being the writer to becoming the editor means that each component has to be scrutinized and looked at objectively to see if the relationship of one part to another makes sense. Each of the various parts should be examined as to the structure that is expected by whatever audiences are in the future.

Readers want to understand what is happening, but they also want to know why it happens. Plus, readers expect to be entertained in the process of following various characters through everyday events. How the pieces fall together and how the events logically flow from each other directly relate to how causes tie to outcomes and prompt other consequences.

Events should have results, or at least show consequences. The number of sidesteps (or missteps) relate to end results. If suspense is increased and the pace of intensity grows, the events are valid. If not, the structure of the plot is weak. When intense action does not build, or is too mundane, there is no threat or there are no life or death decisions to make.

Like archeological digs, edits chart each level from the more scattered down to the narrowly intense bottom levels where resolution takes place with some final reassure or a release from frenzied uncertainty. Structure evolves and is strengthened when plots move from broad scenarios that include different elements to more narrow choices to focus on specifics. Edit to clarify and expand readability of both broader scenes and any specifics included.

Errors or imperfect details are easily overlooked. The whole work should be reflected in the different parts or sections included. When the sections are out of place, or some part is either superficial or not stated adequately, a good examination that questions what is wrong is mandated. What is right can be reinforced or expanded as soon as the need is identified, or the material can be put aside for a later examination if there is some doubt as to the approach necessary to make improvements.

Editing the core of any work implies that all of the critical points are examined to see if they are all necessary and if they are adequate to the plot. Checks are made to assure that precise descriptions are included. All major events should follow logically. Scenes are limited to only those necessary to carry the story. Each section or the components in a section are all tightly described according to the time frame expected.

The core edit should assure that all unnecessary words are deleted and all characters are adequately portrayed or eliminated. When a phrase or section is important, keep it. When it is redundant or adds nothing, change it or take it out.

1. Place or Setting:

Every story takes place in certain locations, with specific people behaving their own way at various times. All of the pieces of every story have limitations, but most writers attempt to honestly describe the movement of people from one place to another. In efforts to enrich the story, most shifts are logical, necessary, and interesting.

Not all such efforts succeed. The editor attempts to verify consistency and strengthen the action of various characters and their movements within the story. The approaches used can be checked, re-checked, and checked again to assure that what is going on is reasonable and needed. When nausea is prompted by all of the reviews, the finish can begin.

The attitude, humor, and the timing of the each dilemma show themselves in the point of view and in the voice used throughout the telling of the story. The writer may switch from using the first person to the third person in some places. When the changes made are important to the point of view, or if the story is made merely adequate by the shifts, an editor may have to decide if changing voice or point of view improves the story and the people included become more real or more interesting. The switch from one voice to another may be simply errors made due to the time elapsed between working on one part and then another.

Objective questioning is not a simple task. Removing parts or just bits and pieces to make the whole work more interesting is tough. Changing the tone of a conversation or describing the attitudes of the people having a disagreement may require a magician's touch. Written material becomes increasingly hard to 'fix' when a section or groups of paragraphs sounds just fine to the writer.

When reading through the various scenes, remember that each scene deserves a beginning, middle, and an end. Structure is not always obvious in different scenes, but structure promotes the theme of each work even when the message is not evident to the writer or to the reader. Without an underlying organization, the writing strays into ramblings. Awareness that each story has a theme that somehow relates to the goal that supports all of the actions and reasons for the story to exist can make it easier to rearrange pieces that may be out of place.

Enough accurate description should be included to pinpoint the locations used in a scene without necessarily skewing the settings or adding filler just to extend the scenes used. Check out the openings of each scene and the closings of scenes for continuity within each section to assure that the readers knows where the people are. The openings and closings may run past one scene and be included in the next scene, but the flow of action should not be disjointed.

As each new location is presented, there should be continuity between the last place and the next, or there should be a complete switch as a new location is presented. The approach used in changing scenes from one location to another is not as important as the accuracy of descriptions used to explain or to let the reader know that a change is made. An awareness that the reader may get lost among what is happening helps an edit clarify location, characters involved, and whose struggle is paramount. All of the parts included should support each other or else they should be eliminated. Some probably need to be tightened or expanded.

Settings and location descriptions can be filler, or they can be critical to the story's plot. Some come across as travel logs. Who ate what at which restaurant or who added what wine to a meal can be dull. Essential location descriptions can add to the moods of various characters or they can excite the reader to want to know more about the places described and the effects created by the smog, the fresh air, the dangers present, or simply the feelings caught when on a particular street. A good rule to follow is to avoid trying to fool anybody about a place that's real when the descriptions are figments of a lazy writer's imagination.

Settings can be detailed or they can be vague and used only as a background for actions depending on what circumstances are tied to the larger plot. Descriptions of various places may be given through dialogue or by general narrative as long as they are accurate. When places are examined as they relate to structure, places may show lack of balance or even have too many diversions that cause cracks in the overall story line.

Places or settings are strong supports to the plot. They can add curiosity to a theme's purpose or there may be too many different places with too many details that distract from the plot, or they may not help lead characters reach their goals. Jumping back and forth between what is taking place elsewhere may keep the action moving but it must be coherent and logical to the story. A caution, however, is needed. Time and place shifts must be understood by readers with typed break indicators, extra spaces, or some method that clearly shows a change.

#2. People:

A review of dialogues used throughout tells the editor/ writer that there is too much sameness among the people included, or that the individuality of each person who speaks is clear. When all of the people who speak sound too much like each other, there is a problem that needs to be fixed.

Hints about the personalities or the moods show through when some idea is given about what is happening to the people talking. Some beginning writers try to include more than two people in a conversation, but it seldom works well. When more than two people talk, the focus needs to shift from only two who are having a conversation to include other people. Transitions that show that different people are included can be short introductions of all the people involved or simply a short mention of some intrusion. The form used is not as critical as showing that others are involved.

Listening is easy for some and not practiced by others. One way to write good dialogue is to listen to how different people talk. Differences in emphasis, in dialect, in abruptness, or shyness can be heard from real people talking about real things. Regionalisms add flavor, but when a cowboy or a farm hand says, "I reckon" too many times, it's tiresome. Dialogue attention getters include strong words. A tough guy or strong character can get away with strong words. A diplomat can hover between appeasement and modified toughness in speech. A woman senator may use pleasant words while she speaks softly yet toughness with an undercurrent of strong ideas can be implied. Statements can be whispered, or a slip of the tongue approach can give away secrets. Every phrase can create suspense or be a good shift between people speaking.

With clear and useful identities, each character should be sustained throughout the story or left out. Honest portrayals of each character reflect a writer's ability to show inner characteristics of different people. Along with inclinations to behave in particular ways, each character must be unique unto themselves. Edit in separate and distinctive behaviors or some physical oddities that highlights each person.

A writer may not realize that a reader can't tell one character from another. Edit sweeps can focus on similarities, but distinctions are useful, and a careful edit helps make each person separately identifiable and necessary to the plot. When a person shows up in the first scene and disappears until the middle or the end scenes, unless they are the missing person who needs to be found, there has to be some clear reason for the long gap or they are not important and can be eliminated altogether.

Characters should be examined to assure that everyone named is important to the plot and that each person included is necessary. When there are too many, a small group or a crowd may be substituted instead of naming one after another who seemed important during the writing process but get in the way during the editing process. When there are too few, the story may be weakened. Too many may be confusing or merely distracting.

Each person can be made memorable or they can fade away. When characters roles either need to be significant or be made more elaborate, or even if some characters need to disappear, changes should be intentional and should strengthen the story. Every person included deserves a hard review as to whether they are distractions or should become more important. Sprinkles of information can be added to add depth and variety to any person's personality.

When a character deserves more than a brief description of what kind of clothes they wear, they probably should be included throughout and mentioned frequently. The kind of thoughts they carry around in their heads may explain why they act the way they do under certain circumstances. If characters support action and test a reader's imagination, repeated appearances are justified. When explanations of thoughts are not included, some other valid reason should be given for behaviors or attitudes that prompt whatever action results.

Team tournaments are a process of elimination. Edits of character structure is a bit like measuring the strengths and weakness of members of a team. Readers should feel the pains and struggles of both likeable and despicable people. As long as characters come across as real, there is support from readers. Bad behavior, illegal acts, criminal deeds and other repulsive acts can all be done by charming, likeable people who can enchant or dismay readers.

Editing character structure implies that each person included is recognizable throughout the story. Readers expect to know the people in every scene, or at least be able to recognize who is where. When someone has no distinguishable characteristics, they are more easily forgotten. When a character goes from one behavior pattern to another, it is confusing unless the changes are explained. People may be good or they may be evil. Mostly, they are consistent and predictable.

Empathy builds in readers when a character's goals, needs, triumphs, hurts, or disappointments are identified. When endowed with human traits, each character included stays longer in a reader's memory. An editor, however, looks for too many frailties in even the toughest hero. Keep a hero balanced between being too powerfully capable and too wishy-washy or full of anger.

Tensions between people add to the drama, or come across as artificial. Some interpersonal tensions may be important, but when they are artificial, they become transparent to readers and promote a sense of disillusionment in the quality of the writing. Writing presented to sophisticated audiences should not come across as tom-foolery.

Substance added to each personality promotes continued interest as long as extra descriptions don't keep expanding to the point of dullness. Secondary characters should not take over and become too dominant, effectively up-staging the lead role that was supposed to go to the hero. Changing descriptions of people, adding strength to their roles, or downplaying their importance in the story can show positive results or create confusion. Edit for plausibility and well displayed human characteristics that showcase each person in their finest as they move through different events.

#3 Plot:

When is a plot not a plot? If there is no reason for something to happen or if the simple goal of a story is missing, there is no discernable plot. A carefully considered decision to explore and explain an idea enables writers to design and present various plots in wide varieties of form and substance.

Vague ramblings and reminiscing get burdensome and interfere with the story and the plot suffers. When psychological introspection takes over and the paths taken by people within the story get lost in confusions, the plot becomes less important than the need to escape to other recreations and so avoid the writings.

Some writers are determined to add as many words as possible to every manuscript they attempt just to continue writing. If writing is only stringing words together, a plot may evolve, or not. It is unlikely that stream-of-consciousness writing is driven by the development of a plot. If there is a purpose to including psychobabble, it may be that the writer continues to expound in writing and listens to an inner voice that no other person hears. Unless a particular character is designed to represent someone in a psychiatric ward, loosely written and internally driven dialogue is meaningless to readers and should be cut.

In order to examine a plot, many points of objectivity become critical to a full and complete review. When the details of a story are stripped away from the plot, structure is more clearly seen. Among the many types of plot, some are simple straightforward stories, others are multi-dimensional and multi-generational. Some plots are thin and scarce on meaningful emotions or insightful elements that reflect on human relationships or even that vaguely support a theme.

When a plot unfolds as the writer intended, it entices the reader's involvement. During a review of the plot's action, an edit may disclose that the momentum or pace is too slow. The question of what happens next is always part of editing the plot components of any significant plot. Observe the consistency of action throughout every examination of plot. If the work starts off with quick action, keep it quick throughout. If the pace of the plot is leisurely or casual, it should remain leisurely and casual throughout. A plot overview can determine that the tempo is steady and constant or that the tempo is uncertain and imbalanced. If an imbalance is discovered through an edit, any unevenness can be corrected.

#4. Purpose:

Facts and descriptions may be interesting and can be made even more so when some of them are deleted or tightened with shorter sentences. Repetitions can be avoided. If information is already provided, it should not be hammered into the readers. With too much redundancy, readers may want the story to hurry along so they can forget all the nonsense in between the present danger and the solution to the next problem. The answer may be to break up the sections and insert some transitions between scenes or settings.

Editing involves an overview of the way scenes support the plot. Each scene can have a focus that is descriptive and a purpose that has meaning. Wherever the scene takes place, there should be a reason for it being where it is. If the location of a scene is valid, the placement of the scene within the story must be valid as well. When a scene is examined in light of its effectiveness, its necessity, its depth, or if it has some other purpose, then it can be strengthened or eliminated or re-positioned to another place within the plot.

To expect a writer to know or to recognize that a scene is effective is almost like asking a non-swimmer to make it across the English Channel without benefit of assistance. The advantage is in the examination process and the degree to which a writer tries to stay objective. Objective writers and critical editors think about readers who may not have the same level of familiarity with the subject as the writer. Readers expect a great deal as they plow through unfamiliar territory.

Moving from being a solitary writer to becoming an analytical editor is almost like becoming a stranger who reads new material for the first time. It may be like walking into a magician's mirror to become someone who wears a different hat, thinks differently, and is not afraid of facing distortions. The switch off of one set of skills in order to adopt another set of skills is difficult but not insurmountable.

'*Ingenious*' is the root word for the now common word '*engines.*' Newly built, replaced, substituted, or upgraded, engines move things and people from one place to another. Ideas are the engines of books. Stories depend on structure to move readers from real worlds into places created by the imagination of writers. Polished by editing and produced by publishers, readers are mentally and/or emotionally moved from their realities into the worlds built by writers. Precise parts, balanced, placed in proper sequences provide countless journeys for multitudes of readers. Every detail influences the effectiveness of the engines and accomplishes the journey.

Experienced writers know better than to drown in the idea of a story that begins as a fascination. A writer may consider an idea only to reject it when it is outlined or examined objectively. Perfectionist writers may find an idea so intriguing, the work may go on and on and never be finished.

A sound approach is to keep the idea short even when it is complicated so that it can be substantially woven throughout the plot or sub-plots. All of the various integrative elements of the work are more easily checked for consistency and clarity in a short idea. 'Short' does not imply simple. Succinct and tightly constructed with ample condensing to provide meaningful examinations better describes a manageable or short idea. When a work is manageable, it is easier to edit and to substantially improve all of the various pieces.

#5. Theme:

Woven among, but underlying all the others, is the theme of the story. Some would put plot in first place, but until all the pieces are described or outlined as to their functions and roles, the theme may stay hidden. The theme of a work may never be disclosed, or it may be stated in the first sentence. An underlying morality of the story may be subtle and known only to the writer, or the unifying message of the entire work become obvious only after close scrutiny.

A focus on theme helps determine whether or not there is an identifiable reason for whatever is happening to support a universal tendency. Some writers use a theme to help structure the plot they choose. Other writers choose to wait to let the end theme be discovered. A few writers subtly allow the theme to fit the needs of readers. Thus, the focus varies with the editor and with the reader.

Critical examination:

A good edit looks for fallacies included in setting descriptions, narrative, or during conversations by different characters. An editor must be alert to disconnections within any part of a chapter or scene, and know when it is time to change a word, a sentence, or an entire section. It is difficult to take an objective approach on how the writing may be corrected, polished, improved, or otherwise made more readable to audiences interested enough in the content to purchase an author's work.

Objective analysis is necessary to thorough editing. How can a writer be objective about the work just produced? Many ways are helpful. None are easy. Getting help from a willing partner who is unafraid to give honest feedback can assist and provide competency. Some writers let the work get cold. After some apparent neglect, or other distractions have intervened, writers come back to the work with a fresh attitude. Often the words can be read as if someone else wrote them and what comes next is a surprise. When picked up after a period of time, mistakes may be obvious or there may be a 'wow' factor that makes a writer wonder how well a piece got written.

Characters may not be distinctive enough or they are so lightly described as to be forgotten. People included in the story can be made into separately distinct individuals by alert editing. They may be reflections of the writer's own persona, or they may be distinctive, but changes won't be made until there is an awareness of the need to fix details.

After the integrative elements of place, people, purpose and plot have undergone a critical examination and consistency and clarity are satisfactory, there are still questions to be answered. The writer has survived the struggle of writing for days and months. Friends and family have completed their seemingly endless days of neglect, what possible other questions need answers? The questions may be no more obvious than the answers found. Keep looking for inconsistencies.

It takes effort to change a word, a paragraph, or an entire scene. It is always difficult to edit one's own work because every writer clearly understands what is meant. The reader, however, may interpret the words quite differently when clarity is lost and meaning escapes into confusion. If the story does not flow logically, the approach used by the writer is seen as ineffective. An editor's job is to recognize flaws and suggest steps to clarify whatever is confusing.

Schopenhauer wrote, "All generalities are false." So are these general statements about editing. Good edits, however, improve and sustain good writing. Layers of each life's story or potential story can be peeled away like wraps of an onion. Edits that peel away various layers of structure complement read-through editing. Select one major component (such as one of the P's) and proceed cautiously.

Personal agendas:

Every person is a book, a story perhaps untold, unwritten except in their own mind's eye. It can be difficult for a writer to avoid interjections of a personal bias or political persuasion into their writing. A personal agenda may be included, but only in such a way as to add to the story and not be an interruption or be too obviously a personal bias on the part of the writer. When it is obvious that there is some personal agenda of the writer's which does not belong to the story, the frequent reaction of readers is that the finished product is quackery and cannot be taken seriously.

When personal agendas or mandates important to the writer interrupt the story and become obvious to the reader, they should be excluded during the editing process. If philosophies, political controversies and other personal vendettas creep into the story, they can be included as a preference of a character or of a group important to the story.

During editing, watch for passages or scenes that come across as morality statements or those that hound the reader to follow a particular political bent. Purpose is paramount. An approach that is too blatant or too extreme can be adjusted. Readers who don't support a particular philosophic or political trend may reject radical approaches and refuse to be an audience. Writing intended as philosophical, theological, psychological, or other informative matter, must also contain facts and objectively state whatever material is chosen.

An editing question to ask and to answer may be: Is the writer careful to take out any hint that the author is coming across to the reader instead of what is happening? Action is a needed part of what is going on but editorials or political pronouncements should be subtle if they are included. Many characters have opinions and add flavor. An edit can identify opinionated people as either necessary or blatantly extraneous. When they add to the impression intended, the writing is strengthened. Otherwise, they can be made quieter or eliminated altogether.

Both non-fiction and fiction inform. Some or both entertain. Many are appropriately inspirational and occasionally awe inspiring. Accuracy in showing ways in which different situations affect the people involved in a story is important to readers, other writers, and to editors, regardless of the type of book developed.

A chapter, section, or the entire story may not make sense until all of the pieces come together. Deletions of seemingly irrelevant sections, paragraphs, sentences, or even single words may create confusions later on. Any possible deletions or changes can be marked for re-consideration without actually making any cuts until a final reading or all reviews are finished. Any portions that must be repaired are identified and probably rescued from oblivion and other mistakes are avoided.

Filler:

The view of the street outside a foggy window may be appropriate filler when used while the main character decides what to do, or if there are suspicious strangers staring up at the window. There may be other reasons to mention the view of the street or the foggy window, but the reasons must be important or the view from inside or outside the window should not be mentioned.

Fillers may be used as stall tactics, diversions, or as a memory jog to prompt a reader's recall of an earlier place or time or event. Filler settings can be used as a means of letting a character figure out what is supposed to come next. Regardless of the reason for using filler, it should reflect the moment in time and location accurately.

It is easy to become lost in structural convolutions when a story wanders around too much for the reader (or the editor) to follow all of the twists and turns, but practice and alertness remain the underpinnings of success.

CHAPTER NINE

Published – A Goal

There is a grain of potential in each of us. If nurtured, potential grows. If trampled on, the grain languishes and perishes.

-B. Franke

Writing is a journey. Ideas evolve into plots. Characters, settings, and action are three cornerstones of every good story. Conceived challenges are presented to interesting characters. Many obstacles are overcome with or without dire consequences. Settings are appropriately interesting and weather changes reflect moods. Dramatic tensions make some readers stay up all night to see what happens next. Rich details elaborate on curious happenings and expanded action includes struggles with unknown dangers, real or imagined. Repeated sweeps and double checks are needed to validate a point that seems unimportant early but what later becomes significant.

Proofreading, copy editing, and final edits are distinct steps that support each other and lead toward a final manuscript that may not be finished until an agent or a publishing house editor agrees that is it completed. Focused only on what has been done is insufficient. The end may be just over the horizon, but the determination needed to continue until the finish is reached may falter or wane. Many writers give up and store old manuscripts along with their visions of being published and becoming an author. Specific steps, however, can be taken to smooth the paths toward destinations that some see as too difficult to attempt.

Once the various pieces are compiled, the time has come to let the material stand on its own and the search begins for an agent who knows how to work with publishers. Writer who traveled through their aspirations to success have found persistence valuable, but stubborn wishing alone is insufficient. Know what to expect and how publishers make decisions and the paths can be shortened.

Writers can spend so much time involved in the process of writing they forget about readers. Decades ago, Bennet Cerf wrote in his anthology, <u>Reading for Pleasure</u>, the following:

"Statistics reveal that a million or so more American are 'reading for pleasure' every year, although you never would believe this by listening to the moans of the publishing fraternity. Publishers cry more readily than anybody else on earth. A simple, routine inquiry like 'How's business?' is enough to make their tears flow like water, diluting their vintage wines and drenching the decks of their private yachts.

"To hear them tell it, there's always something threatening to bankrupt half the publishers in America. Seventy years ago, believe it or not, a spokesman for the industry predicted that interurban trolly cars would be the doom of the reading

habit! So many people were swinging and swaying aboard these dangerous contraptions that there soon would be nobody left to appreciate Shakespeare and Aristotle!

"Then came the menace of the bicycle, followed closely by cheap automobiles, magazines, giant economy-size Sunday newspapers, motion picture, radio, and now, of course, television.

"Anybody fortunate enough, however, to have learned the joys of reading in his formative years—usually through the inspired guidance on one wise, gratefully remembered, and disgracefully under-paid schoolteacher—knows that there never has been, and never will be a substitute for a really good book. All the wisdom of the ages, all the tales that have delighted mankind for generations, are there at your fingertips, at negligible cost, to be picked up, savored, digested, and laid down exactly as your fancy dictates. That's why more good books are sold in America every season, despite all other gimmicks and distractions."

People keep reading, writers keep writing, and good books get published by highly selective publishers irrespective of the costs. Moving from being a 'writer' to being an 'author' is almost as complicated as learning how to move from being a writer to being an editor. A *writer* continues to write regardless of how many or how few publishers are interested in printing any of the writer's work. An *author* is one who has negotiated contracts, is published, and accomplished what many writers long for and that is to see a finished product grace the shelves of bookstores.

Traditional publishing houses, or trade publishers as they are sometimes called, print and distribute books for wide publics and general reading. Academic texts or those prepared for professional fields are generally produced by specialized publishers. Historically, a few select publishers decided who and what was bought from well connected or highly recognized agents who sponsor qualified writers. Currently, more publishing options are available, but most are still highly selective in the acceptance of new writers.

Self-publishing is widely available. Vanity presses abound and publish works paid for by authors. Distribution and advertising promotions may be provided, but they also are paid for by authors. Many famous authors start their paths toward being published by using the self-published approach. It is a grand teaching tool with quality people who spend endless hours coaching newcomers about the technical side of moving a 'finished' product through to the printed stage. Self-publishing is paid for by the writer, of course.

With all of the technological advances, writers have more choices than in past years, but the pathways remain similar. The world-wide web has published serials and chapter-by-chapter versions of both newcomers and famous writers. Print-on-demand publishing is growing and may become the next wave in book creation.

Small press editions are printed in every size and category. College and University presses try to focus on their own faculty members, but occasionally add outsiders to their limited edition publications. Regional or statewide presses cite their preferences and most knowledgeable writers do not waste time pursuing out of state or out of region publishers when it is inappropriate to do so.

Most agents and most publishing houses would rather receive a query letter and/or a synopsis as first steps in the process. It is easier for both agent and publisher to peruse a brief proposal than to plough through hundreds of pages only to decide the style of the writer or the focus of the work does not meet the publisher's schedule or their target audiences.

Synopsis:

Some writers outline before they start writing. Other writers begin writing and wait to see how it will all turn out. To prepare an outline of every scene is time consuming and considered by many writers to be dull and unnecessary. Other writers prepare detailed outlines of each scene and find the entire effort highly valuable. It is easier to discard one long page of notes than to revise a manuscript that has lost its way in the minutiae.

Some call the synopsis an outline. Others call the synopsis a review or even a 'brief.' Whatever term is used, a synopsis of the total work along with three sample chapters *may* be enough to get an agent to pursue a publisher who *may* consider going forward toward the last steps involved in having a published product.

A synopsis must be exciting. Mood, intent of action, and concern for whatever audience there may be should be reflected in a brief overview of the whole manuscript. Information from a publisher may become a guide, but doing a synopsis forces a writer to have a concise understanding of both organization and content. Occasionally a synopsis causes changes to be made in the organization of the material before it is sent out to the larger world.

Without giving away the surprise ending, briefly tell what the book is about. Capture the movement within the story as it unfolds, but stay away from too many details. The finished work will have all of the details included as needed, but publishers want to know the vital points in the final work and not be burdened with unnecessary details. One way to prepare a synopsis is to condense and then condense again. Keep each part of a synopsis as tight as possible. Extra words do not make good copy in a tight synopsis and may fail to add intrigue to a future buyer who only scans what may be the best writing since writing began. To write briefly yet completely is tough. Preparing a short version of key points in a long work is tougher. Keep taking out extraneous material until there is no fluff left and a good synopsis will be the result.

An example of an excellent synopsis is Dr. Ladell Payne's notes from a group discussion he led on Faulkner's <u>Light in August</u>. The title used for his notes was "A Little More Light in August." Although not originally intended to be a synopsis, Dr. Payne agreed to have it included here. Obviously, William Faulkner had no part of this summary.

Synopsis
<u>Light in August</u> – Wm. Faulkner

"The novel, <u>Light in August</u>, is organized around the life journeys of two characters, Joe Christmas, who cannot live in either a white or a black world, and Lena Grove, a paragon of goodness who is pregnant and unwed. The two never meet yet stand symbolically in opposition to each other. Their closest point of contact occurs when Lena first enters the small town of Jefferson and sees smoke from the burning house where Christmas has just murdered his mistress Joanna Burden who's imagined pregnancy contrasts with Lena's actual one.

Lena's story is a comedy in that she affirms values essential to the meaningful continuation of life. She embodies values of humility, good humor, simplicity, innocence, an acceptance of her condition as the Lord's provenance and, above all, a commitment to being a nurturing mother of her unborn child. Her journey to find a father for her child is directly related to her role as a sustaining mother.

Joe Christmas, the result of an illegitimate union, is tragic in that he rejects the sustaining qualities of life and eventually seeks death. Unlike Lena, to whom sex is simply a part of life, Joe sees sex as foul and polluted. As a teenager, Joe is infatuated with Bobbie, a prostitute working as a waitress. Joe performs a ritual animal sacrifice to insure that his woman will be pure and untainted. When he finds out that Bobbie is not, he vomits.

Other characters exist between the values of Lena and those of Joe. Undergirding Joe's destructiveness is the perverted Calvinism of crazed Doc Hines who preaches the superiority of the white race, proclaims that sex is abomination and bitchery, insures that his grandson Joe is "a nigger" and strives to see Joe hanged.

The Reverend Gil Hightower, the Presbyterian minister who has no sexual involvement with the wife who he married in order to gain the pulpit in Jefferson, preaches not the gospel of love and compassion but about his grandfather, a confederate soldier who died gloriously on a galloping horse. Hightower eventually faces the truth of his grandfather's death, who actually dies while trying to rob a chicken house. Lena Grove suggests a pagan Virgin Mary. Joe Christmas becomes a kind of Anti-Christ."

A synopsis offers a condensed summary of what key elements the story holds without criticisms or biased comments. Agents, publishers, or readers draw their own conclusions as to merit, popularity, or market success of each work that carries itself beyond the synopsis. Getting others in the publishing business involved in the writing and in the story is the goal of a synopsis. In common publishing parlance, the synopsis contains the "hook" that catches the attention of those who decide on accepting a piece of writing at a publishing house.

Five lines or less:

Editing does not stop with perusal of lengthy works. A double-spaced synopsis sent to an agent who has enough current contacts to effectively 'peddle' the story may get the attention of a potential advocate. Edit the synopsis. Edit a brief cover letter. Include word count of attached materials and a short 'pitch' summary of live lines or less. Never call the five-line summary a 'pitch.' Every quality agent will recognize the summary for what it is.

Putting together a five (5) line summary of the story is a great help to the writer and to the agent who wants to market the story to future publishers for the general public. When all of the elements are strengthened, or at least included, the big question of how to summarize the plot in five lines or less can be tackled.

A challenging exercise that clarifies the intent of the story line, a five line summary is intended to entice future audiences to take a look at what the story tells. The process of simplifying and putting different words together to say what the story intends to say pushes even experienced writers to know the plot they offer to the world. Without going into detail, summarize the whole effort. The five line description may change many times before it is read by anyone but the writer, but it is a valuable exercise nonetheless.

The few sentences used in an ad to tweak an audience's interest in seeing a movie or to buy a particular digital video disc (DVD) can be a guide to how to proceed. Think of the five-line ads that entice viewers to see a particular movie. A writer who can describe the plot envisioned in five-lines or less has met a challenge.

If the final five lines are used, they may grace the published book on the back cover, on the dust jacket, or perhaps on a placard inside a book store. Agents tend to appreciate a writer's efforts to help prepare future copy for advertising or promotional purposes.

Agents:

Materials sent to an agent and then on to publishers should meet the standards of the targeted publisher. Potential manuscripts and support materials must pass the scrutiny of experienced agents. Most publishers have guidelines which they prefer to send only to agents and most publishers will not accept manuscripts except from qualified agents. Many writers do not have agents. A catch-twenty-two or circular dilemma presents itself. There are many reference books available to guide a search for a reputable agent in every writer's vicinity.

Literary agents and literary agencies come in different sizes with differing styles. Some agents have staff editors to assist in selection of manuscripts deemed publishable. Other agents have ad-hoc editors available to them and many charge a writer for manuscript reviews before the agent will accept the writer as a client.

A few literary agents are independent of any one agency and will contract separately with specific writers and seek to move quality works toward being published. Independent agents are exceptions to the general rule, however, and are not always the recommended way to go unless a writer is looking for pre-publication editing, or other kinds of assistance in moving forward.

Managing the critical step of finding an agent may be the first of many rejections to come, or it may lead to a path of blissful success. Whatever the conclusion, every benefit can accrue to heeding whatever advice is given by an agent. Some agents have ad-hoc editors available to them and will charge a writer for having a manuscript reviewed in-house before an agent will accept the writer as a client. In that literacy agencies function as screening guards for major publishing houses, their guidance and suggestions are critical. When an agency rejects a proposal or does not accept a writer as a client, it does not mean the work can't be improved or that it will not be accepted by another agency.

The process of finding a good representative with good connections in the publishing field simply may take longer and require more persistence along with more copies sent to agents or more e-mails before any confirmations are received. Meanwhile, keep editing and polishing the different pieces of the total work since response times from agents may take several weeks or months.

Once a writer is accepted as a client by the agent, typical agent costs range from fifteen per cent (15%) upwards to twenty five per cent (25%) of whatever income is generated by the agent on behalf of the writer. Other than any up-front fees mutually decided upon for pre-submission preparations, or post-publication marketing or advertising, an agent spends an extraordinary amount of time and effort to push a writer towards success in the marketplace. Each agent negotiates with the publisher to review specifics in each publishing contract including time deadlines, percentages of royalties, printing, and distributions or other tangibles on behalf of the author.

Guidelines:

Guidelines vary from publisher to publisher. Compliance is easier and saves a lot of time and trouble when specific guidelines are followed early in the writing process. Think final edits and make sure guidelines are available at about the same time that a first draft is nearing completion. Experienced writers seek out publisher guidelines before starting more than a cursory edit of a final work.

Some agents have copies of various publisher guidelines, others do not. To facilitate the receipt of a hard-copy of guidelines directly from the publisher, many writers request a copy of guidelines and enclose a self-addressed stamped envelope (SASE). Other writers depend on computer visuals to study specific guidelines from an individual publishing house.

It pays to check out details. Many publishers use industry standards in such details as *underlining*, or the use of *italics* and 'quotation' marks. Some publishers prefer em-dashes over double dashes, others insist that an ellipsis () be used instead of a double dash. Guidelines often include such basic rules as what layout is required, what software is acceptable, and specifics on formatting such as how many spaces to use with indents. Some publishers may not allow indented first paragraphs in each chapter. Others choose to re-format each manuscript according to their own specifications.

Page size and body copy size may be left up to the writer to decide. Occasionally, the publisher has specific sizes for each genre they handle and adjust their royalty contracts and the final price of each volume according to the title, the author, and the potential market for each title.

'Book Doctors' rarely function as agents after they polish a writer's work to make it marketable and a separate agent may be required before approaching a publishing house. 'Book Doctors' and 'Ghost Writers' have varied fee structures, but both usually are paid by the writer. A 'Book Doctor' usually works on prepared drafts. A 'Ghost Writer' may work from interviews, raw notes, or reference documents and never be acknowledged for all of the work that goes into preparing a document for publication.

Rejections:

Rejections do not deter the strong of heart. Over the past decades, many well-published and highly acclaimed authors were repeatedly told they did not have a manuscript that was to be published. Eventually, probably through persistence, they became widely read. Some started out by printing their own work.

The old adage, "you can't tell a book by its cover" no longer applies to the book industry. Modern papers feel enticing. Computer designed covers and logos are sophisticated. Cover stock papers combine with professionally prepared layouts rival major ad agencies in their preparations. Some books fly off shelves because they have customer appeal. Both self-publishing houses and established traditional publishers provide both hard-copy editions complete with dust-covers and soft-cover copies that are perfect-bound. Libraries seldom buy any but hard-copies for the sake of durability.

Most publishers provide copyright holding and file an International Standard Book Number (ISBN) with the Library of Congress. Typically, it takes a long time for official notification of the copyright and the ISBN to be sent to the author.

Most established publishers want to contract with sure winners in the market place in order to cover their costs and assure profit on investments, especially when an author commands a substantial advance and a sizeable percentage of royalties earned. The writer's agent negotiates advances (if any) and royalty rates.

Without necessarily thinking about what is expected, many professional editors tend to ask themselves various questions when they evaluate a manuscript (in hard-copy or from a computer file) before a final decision is made as to whether or not the work is worth publishing. Decision-making agents and/or publisher editors can decide to reject a manuscript or they can wait and let their first impressions fade. If another review is worth their time, they still may have questions that determine acceptance or rejection.

Cautions:

Editors and future readers expect a flow of imagery easily followed. Absorbed by entrancements of action or disconcerted by made-up words or skips in following what is happening make a difference in the quality of the story and its characters. Awkward phrases, strange punctuations, misspelled words, or unique statements that only the author understands can throw readers off the pace of the writing and can interrupt involvement in the story.

Cause and effect are helpful when examining a document for tensions included or omitted. Structural flaws may be caught when an overview is done, or they may not be obvious enough to the writer and depend on the eagle eyes of a professional editor to be pointed out. Either way, examining structure is a necessary part of edit reviews. Every story benefits from sharp editing tools that form the final details and polish each part.

Standards, rules, or simple guides are beneficial when refining a story as it unfolds or as it is handed to others to publish. It is absolutely necessary to improve any writing before it is released to anyone, especially to an agent or to a professional publisher's editorial group.

Many great works are deeply indebted to astute editors. Writers read. Their thirst for quality material with varying concepts abound. Some beginning writers analyze what they read. What genre they read depends on personal tastes. The genre they write usually depends on experiences and interests. Many editors get into the habit of analyzing what they read. Because editors read volumes of material, they may specialize in particular genres in order to have base knowledge of what is accurate and what needs refinements or deletions.

When writers choose to be their own editor, they try to shift gears and put on an analyst hat. Often it works. Sometimes, it doesn't, but there is always a need to continue the process.

CHAPTER TEN

At Last: An Editor

*"It is no use saying, 'We are doing our best.
You have got to succeed in doing what is
necessary'."*
-Prime Minister, Winston S. Churchill

The story may describe interesting places and include fascinating behaviors of various people, but editing involves a critical approach and demands that the writer stay removed from the plots and sub-plots. An editor maintains an awareness of form, structure, the mechanics of writing and the presentations used that make up the whole of the story. Sanjay Sanghoee wrote: "When I first sat down to write <u>Merger</u> I thought that creating a novel was a one-man show. It is not. Writing is one thing. Editing is quite another. The latter deserves a medal of honor." (a TOR Book, N, Y., N Y., 2006, Acknowledgements page.)

Some of the best advice an instructor can give a beginning artist is to know when to stop. The painter pauses over the last stage of polishing the scene and wants to give the newly formed landscape one last brush stroke. Like a painter, a writer often feels the finish is never complete. Some writers find that they harbor a persistent need to fix some real or imagined minor flaw. Most practiced writers continue editing their own work until all of the flaws that are discovered have been corrected. Readers may never know the many sacrifices made throughout the various writing, proofreading, editing processes, but levels of quality show in the final product.

Editorial quality continues past the point when a manuscript is deemed ready to send to anyone appropriate. Suggestions for revisions, clarifications, deletions, or other modifications may come as a surprise to any writer. Each comment from an agent, however, must be taken with gracious acceptance even when wild disagreement with the need for any change is paramount. Resistance toward advice interferes with quality and delays progress.

Overly confident writers may have no concept of how long it takes to move from an idea to the reality of having a manuscript finished and then published. When deadlines are set, disappointments tumble one after the other to beg the question of when one section or another can be completed. Unrealistic deadlines may not be met, but may spur on confusion, disappointments, and cause other untoward pain. On the other hand, more realistic deadlines and advanced planning tend to even out uncertainty and solve many unforeseen problems before they overtake creative urges. Realistic deadlines also help determine what costs to the writer are involved.

Deadlines to spur on the writing and editing process are set whenever possible. Questions arise but steps are taken and decisions made as to how to meet immediate and long term goals. Realistic deadlines used as guides to complete each step are similar to learning to walk or to talk when very young. Struggles abound and some deadlines may be only wishful thinking. Dreams do not take into account all the little disruptions that life brings.

Most first or even second drafts are wobbly. False steps are taken and garbled sentences emerge before strong sure progress can be made. Artificial deadlines can act as incentives and spur acts of completion. Habits are powerful but can get in the way of progress or speed the completion along. Editing to look at faulty steps is almost the same as assurance that habits can be overcome. Accidents or mistakes (taken as inevitable) need editing to provide safety nets through rewriting, revisions, and polishing after the core idea is presented.

One of the more helpful approaches used to finding out where any section, paragraph, or description needs improvement is to put the work down for a while and then pick it up later while trying to think *outside* the role of writer. Another tactic is to use the 'friendly stranger' approach. Give the work to a creditable person who is willing to make specific comments on various sections or to point out details that need to be corrected or improved. New writers sometimes forget that outside comments are about *the work* and not about the person writing the work.

Writers get weary of pushing and pulling and shaping different pieces and parts while the hope for an end seems futile. When the review and editing process takes too long, the subject chosen gets more skewed. At times, it is hard to recall the excitement of starting the process of writing when the beginning flowed beyond the words.

Discouragement comes silently and inhibits the need to continue. Success comes not from accepting weariness or giving in to fatigue. Rather, success comes from overcoming whatever sense of drudgery impedes the determination to finish and be done. At times, the process includes collecting letters of rejection until the whole is polished and ready to be accepted by professionals. Even after a writer edits and submits through an agent, the waiting may seem interminable. Each step in the publishing process requires advanced planning. Expect at least six months before a finished book is released. The many self-publishing firms have their own schedules.

Writers with persistence manage delays and stumble past obstacles. Revisions and corrections assure that mechanical difficulties and errors have been checked and re-checked. Grammatical mistakes have been reviewed and revised. Capitalizations, hyphenations, one word sentences and ellipses that trailed off and left broken thoughts have been changed and fixed.

Persistence means that the writer has compressed, expanded, rearranged, deleted, inserted, clarified and corrected mistakes until there is more than one full waste basket filled with changes discarded. Steadfast scrutiny of any work leads to completion. When writers stay the long, convoluted course of falling only to get up and polish again and again can find reasonable satisfaction in the efforts made. Writers who evolve into editors (of their own work or that of others) become champions of well-formed and thoroughly scrutinized works.

Quality assurances are satisfied when writer/editors have met the challenges to locate vagueness, and to find and improve any contradictions in every written conversation and description. All events within the story have been integrated and actions taken are detailed enough for the reader to understand and follow the sequences intended.

Whenever the work is polished sufficiently, the time has come to seek professionals who can move the work toward actually being published. Agents may ask for additional changes and accept only certain standards from the writers they represent. Editors at publishing houses expect knowledgeable approaches to be taken by the agents they accept. Remember that not all editors are alike and each field has unique approaches and expectations.

Newspaper editors may expect to have to rewrite the notes received from 'stringers' who prepare rough stories of events in the field but rely on the news editors to polish the sketchy facts to fit the designated space in the newspaper. The unique and specialized fields of newspaper writing and news editing are professions all their own. The news editor's approach is separate from and different than that used in editing essays, short stories, novellas, text books, and other literary writings, fiction or non-fiction. Newspaper reviews of new book releases are important to new writers, and the newspaper field must be understood.

Editors vary in their approach. Some newspaper editors expect to do a total re-write as long as the "idea" of the writer is kept. Ordinarily it is not the job of a publisher's editor to re-write a manuscript, nor is it usually an editor's job to write additional material or add to an author's work. But both happen. An editor's job at most major publishing houses is to be aware of the intent of their writers but not to fall into the old trap of doing re-writes. Helpful beyond comparison, however, will be suggestions and comments about particular details professional editors can accept.

Editors carry needs, fears, motives and other personal attitudes around with them and they expect no less from the characters included in any writing they encounter.

Awake or asleep, when a person appears in a story, they potentially become stick figures easily forgotten, or they may be so elaborately displayed they 'take over' and dominate all that surrounds them.

Heroes are fallible. Villains often are attractive people with appealing personalities. Village idiots are clever. Stereotypes are unacceptable to quality writers. Frail editing is inexcusable to the preparation of substantial manuscripts no matter how short or long the finished product.

Writing relies on language combined with intuition, creativity, and imagination. During editing, with the task of revisions in mind, thoughts switch back and forth between identifying spontaneous creation and checking rules of language. Editing the story requires that inspirations be identified, that colorful feelings are included, that the attitudes reflected make sense, and that the flow of dialogue is realistic to the people talking. The edit process also demands examination of the story's logic and analyses of the words used.

The writer/editor's job is to look for and impose clarity of intent into each sentence. This can be done through objectivity and thoroughness provided the audience is kept in mind. Consider the following when trying to find an agent or a publisher:

1. Are the sections logically presented ?
2. Are the type styles distracting or are they easy to read?
3. Are the words too repetitive or is the repetition needed for emphasis or clarity?
4. Are there too many 'frills' included that become distractions?

Query letters, five-line pitches, synopses, or other communications each need to be edited. Tight, concise writing is difficult but is usually respected.

When considering audience, both writer and editor must anticipate what effect the story and the words used can have on readers. Each writer and each reader's experiences are different. Somewhere and somehow the experiences or expectations of both must meet, or else the market is missed and the work may go unpublished. For example, religious books do not contain foul language; romance novels contain explicit descriptors, travel descriptions focus on scenic and physical distinctions. Specifically targeted readers help focus the approach.

Avoid reader confusion regardless of the type of writing to be done, or the type of story to be told. Professional editors know that readers judge both writing style and content. Both must be intriguing and satisfy curiosity about material presented as well as arouse some kind of emotional response in readers. Satisfied readers search for more of the same writer's works. Dissatisfied readers frequently reject the style used by a particular writer and never buy that writer's work again.

Examining the presentation of minor parts or looking at the entirety pushes both the determination of the editor and the creativity of the writer to work in tandem. It's easier when the writer's creativity and the editor's analysis work together and switch back and forth with each section changed as needed. The edit process sees that this or that needs to be corrected or changed. The writing process goes ahead and makes whatever corrections are needed. When only one task can be undertaken at a time, it is customary to push the writing as far as it can be taken before the editing comes into play. Different approaches are valid.

Editing requires alertness and includes questions. The difficult question of 'What is wrong here?' is asked frequently. Answers may not be immediately apparent. The story may be interrupted by excessive distractions such as when descriptions of bad roads or foul weather interrupt an important sequence. At times there may be too many sidelines interjected such as how many headaches Aunt Gussie endures. Once some answers are found, only information that is relevant needs to remain. Everything else can be condensed or removed.

The quality or validity of a work may relate to instructional guides that are repetitive in nature, or may be relative to literary or commercial works. Talent is a much admired quality regardless of the form it takes. Much like the seed that bursts forth from a glorious plant that withers and dies without moisture and balanced nutrients, talent often ceases to flourish. Both internal and external strengths must be nourished in order for quality talent to persist.

Editors know good writing when it is presented. When the rules or standards are broken, there must be good reasons or valid rationales and purpose behind the exceptions used. Excuses of individual preferences or creative expression become obvious and may lead to rejection. Poor form disguised as ingenuity seldom benefits either the writer or the reader.

Too much polish can be a distraction since some writing tends to never end. Writers have been known to continue to polish ad infinitum and never complete the manuscript they started. The tendency to perfect each and every word is a great asset but the overly concerned approach to keep adding or to keep changing becomes a detriment to completion. Writers who strike a balanced approach and know when to turn their efforts over to someone accomplished in editing are more likely to complete a work than those who continually struggle to 'fix' something that has already been corrected.

Too little polish may smack of laziness or incompetence. Sections that jump the story ahead of itself or leave bare places require polish. What does 'jumps the story ahead of itself' mean? Perhaps too many secrets are exposed too soon and the end becomes evident. Perhaps one character becomes too dominant and takes over the place of the character who was intended to be the lead hero.

When sentences seem too familiar to the reader, the computer may have inserted a paragraph more than once. Or, the section was written on a Tuesday and forgotten about by the following week. Perhaps an event was explained earlier or included under a different pretext in some other section of the work. Repetitions that drive home a point or add emphasis are acceptable, but unintentional word-for-word repeats, are errors.

Polishing a work is almost, but not quite, the same thing as editing one's own work. The difference comes in trying to stay objective while still being involved in the story during the polish stage. It is not always possible to see patterns that need to be improved, nor is it always possible to find descriptions which may interfere with action if the story is foremost in the mind of the writer. Writers who are impatient to get to the publishing stage tend to overlook critical steps in getting the attention they expect.

Professional editors are not interested in raw and unfinished works. Many copies of finely tuned manuscripts pile up and destroy the harried schedules of editors. The selection process of any well written and finely edited manuscripts may rest on the difference of what is interesting and what is dull reading.

Guidelines:

Every publishing house has standards and expectations of what is expected of writers and willingly provide guidelines to agents and to individuals on request. Other elements come into play, but most editors ignore manuscripts that are outside the area of their intent to publish. It is the responsibility of writers and agents to know the specific markets of a publishing house prior to contact.

Sending unsolicited material is usually a great waste of time and effort unless there is an overt statement in a publisher's guidelines that clearly states that unsolicited material from new writers will be considered. Precise information on format, timing of acceptance notices, and length of waiting periods to receive acknowledgements vary. Publisher editors are busy people and seldom appreciate getting the pounds of paper that represent an unsolicited manuscript, especially when furnished guidelines emphasize that no manuscript will be accepted unless it is provided by an agent who has thoroughly screened the material. Most publishers won't bother to read or even respond to a manuscript that comes to them uninvited.

Both agents and publishers ordinarily expect that a standard manuscript format be followed although there is no single physical format required by all. Common features of the standard manuscript format include that the left, right, and bottom margins be at least one and one-half inches each. Ink must be dark. Double spacing is necessary. Never staple or bind pages together. Always use white paper that is standard eight and a half by eleven inches in size.

Query Letters:
Regardless of the type of story presented, specifically provided guidelines must be followed carefully. Both agents and publishing staff also expect a well written (and well edited) letter of inquiry before the written material will be considered. If interested, certain chapters or the full manuscript will be requested. If not interested, the agency contacted usually sends their own rejection letter or postcard, or a copy of any rejection notices from publishers will be forwarded to the writer.

After all of the efforts made in writing a lengthy document, and all parts of the work have been examined many times, and all necessary (or obvious) changes have been made, more looming questions rise. Now what must be done? How does the lonely and tiresome task of putting all those words together finally move into the public arena? Important people need to know about the work and its importance to the writer.

Introductions must be made. The idea behind what is said, or the genre of the work needs to be explained and the effort again must be made to allow others to scrutinize the finished product.

In business, a letter of introduction is expected to open doors for the person being introduced. In publishing parlance, a letter of introduction is called a 'query.' It is tempting to send a synopsis or a few sample chapters, or examples of other published writing. Resist temptations. Save time, copier ink, postage, and other costly considerations and develop a cohesive and persuasive *letter of introduction* to the product just completed. Add an enlightening summary of credentials along with the *one page* sales letter if there is no space left in the condensed introduction of the story. The entire story may be shared later if the agent or editor is interested.

Bio information can be included in the one page letter, or proudly stated credentials can be attached. Either way, a compelling introduction of writer and a description of the work produced must be brief. *Edit before sending* is a must for any and all correspondence.

When seeking representation, send the letter to an agent, not to publishing houses. Agents appreciate brevity along with clarity. Pitch the work along with some highlights about the writer, but do not drown the agent's schedule with too much unnecessary stuff. It only takes a few minutes for a significant person in an agency to reject the pounds of inquiries received in any one day's mail or in the hundreds of e-mails received. Be powerfully succinct. Agents who respond favorably to the query may well forward the same letter to their best contact in a publishing house.

If contact with publishers is a goal, send the query letter to only those who do not require contact by an agent or those who will accept unsolicited manuscripts. Research and discover only publishers who are realistic targets before sending anything.

Anxiety over the possibility of meeting success is common. Spurred by anxiety, efforts to 'sell' an idea for a book can be premature and lead to sending both agents and publishers query letters. Such a broad search for support is a waste of time. Forget it. Finish the writing. Do the editing. Make the corrections and then write the query.

Do NOT pester agents with unnecessary telephone calls or e-mail questions or reminders that an important work is on its way or that a silent non-response is overwhelming.

People (agents or editors attached to publishing houses) who get interested in what they find in a query letter expect to see the entire work when they ask for it. Prompt readiness to ship of an entire *boxed but unbound* manuscript is not the end of anxiety. More revisions and additional editing should be expected. Most new writers work hard on revisions suggested by either agent or publisher or both. Some agents will expect the revisions to be made before the manuscript is forwarded to the publishing house. Follow the lead of recommendations made and ignore anxiety responses.

First impressions are significant. Most strong first impressions linger and are not forgotten. A query letter is more than just a request for consideration. It is a first impression introduction not to be taken lightly. The high level of professionally polished writing in the letter of inquiry is probably as important as the first or last chapters of the work the writer hopes to have published. But, write the novel first! Edit each page carefully! Never promise an agent or a publisher that a manuscript is on its way until the last edit has been done and the last sentence is finished.

Just as movie or screen play producers "pitch" stories to potential funding sources, the query letter is the "pitch" that hooks the potential publishers and increases the chances of drawing in the funds and a published work. Without being cute, the author is introduced. Credentials should be crisp and not ego-driven. Briefly include all published tomes and include educational levels as appropriate. Agents and publishing house personnel want to know who the person is that has taken on the long and lonely task of writing a particular work.

Here is where the polished synopsis fits. The plot is introduced with only the main characters and the most critical points of the story. Since query letters are single spaced, the synopsis may fit well or it may need to be condensed further.

Marketing:

Photos of the writer may require professional photographers, but this process may be among the last steps taken. Plans to sell the product developed through the hard work of many people is a special and separate exercise that takes place in the future but is planned and prepared in the present. Select markets are competitive and costs are always a consideration. Agents and publishers expect writers to know who their primary targets of readers are, and how many general audience readers may buy the book.

Promotion efforts on the part of agents and publishers wane without participation from the writer. Support from each are vital to on-going involvement in public appearances, presentations to clubs and other groups, and being available to different audiences. After many months of edits, and finally having a finished and published work, sales of a final product is a worthy goal reached through persistent attention to each small detail.

Long before a writer reaches the point of presenting any writing to a professional editor, there are many guides to help prepare against <u>rejection.</u>

Once the early drafts are done and prepared as completely as possible, questions still arise and the willingness to do a good job of editing is necessary although not always welcomed.

The last review:

All the questions an edit attempted to resolve were reviewed and answered, but lingering doubts remain.

1. What inconsistencies were found? Were they grammatical or structural? Were they intentional or merely computer generated flaws?
2. Was the plot creditable?
3. Were the descriptions necessary or just fluff?
4. Were there too many gaps? Were the gaps filled?
5. Was the point of view the most appropriate for the story being told? Did the point of view shift on purpose?

Answered questions still raise doubts. Start over. Take a look at reader acceptance or reactions.

1. Is the main character likeable? Does the reader care what happens? Are all the people included necessary?
2. Are all of the characters distinct individuals?
3. Is the dialogue believable?
4. Is the action and suspense high drama, adequate, weak, or missing?
5. Are there extraneous ramblings which add little?
6. Is the writing disjointed?
7. Are sequences or sections out of place?
8. What can be cut out?
9. What needs to be expanded or explained better?
10. Is the writing polished and professional?

When a person reads a book, they want to follow the train of thought presented through the written word and through the organization of thoughts. Readers expect to follow whatever ideas are presented, to be able to visualize the places described, and to be able to recognize and understand what is happening as the printed pages unfold a journey.

Readers can either lose themselves in the ideas and visions presented to them, or they can get restless and become impatient trying to follow the concepts laid out in the descriptions, action, or details. A reader must be able to see the same word-pictures as the writer who prepared the work. A finished document stands alone and is either accepted or rejected.

One last reminder: Keep writing!

Consider the points in EDITING – 10 Steps as a guide to both new and experienced writers who want to polish their own work before handing it off to a teacher, an agent or to a publisher.

Reactions to the process of examining EDITING – 10 Steps conclude that it is "a good (perhaps great) resource book."

EDITING – 10 Steps is a solid reference book to be used over and over during the many days usually needed to write anything of significance.

A published author, free-lance editor, and speaker, Dr. Franke earned her Ph.D. from the University of Alabama, Tuscaloosa. She lives in Plano, Texas.